What State Are We In

Six forms of Statehood

Three-dimensional Concept of Society

Four + One Social Orders

**Aimwell 2019

Title: What State Are We In

Subtitle: Six forms of statehood, Three-dimensional concept of society, Four + One social orders

Author: Paul Tammert

Copyright © Paul Tammert

Publisher Aimwell Ltd, Luha 21, Tallinn, Estonia, 10131

First published printed book in the Estonian language 2017

Original Estonian title: Poliitilised valikud türannia ja heaoluühiskonna vahel

First published e-book in the Estonian language 2018

Original Estonian title: Millist riiki?

Translation to english: Tiina-Kaia Ets and E-Koolituse Ltd

https://p2pkoolitus.ee/e-raamatud/

Estonian editor: Eha Karlep

Cover design, illustrations: Marje Tammert

English editor: James Ryan

The First Publication 9.2019.

ISBN 978-9949-7312-1-3 (epub)

Table of contents

AUTHOR'S FOREWORD

Dear reader! This book has come to fruition as a result of nearly 30 years of research and thought. This work arose from a unique event that I and all my contemporaries experienced – the collapse of a state. Although every person and every society are constantly engaged in finding responses to the situations they encounter in life and seeking suitable solutions to the problems that arise, few have the good fortune of starting from a "blank page". The experience that the people of Estonia and Eastern European states who regained their independence underwent while constructing their new state was exceptionally educational – particularly when one compares the development of each state with that of the others. All kinds of development were possible, at least theoretically.

Time and again, the citizens of Estonia raise the question: "Is this really the state we wanted?" However, when we have asked people what kind of state they actually want, we have not received a single clear answer. Populist slogans like "a caring state" are downright criminal, because they create the illusion that somewhere there exists someone with limitless resources, but is too stingy to share them with the people. If we replace the word "state" in this slogan with the word "government", it loses its attractiveness, because "a caring government" must start imposing higher taxes to advance its welfare services...and that is no longer "sexy"!

This gives rise to the question: "What kind of state do we really want for ourselves?" If we rate the choices made by the states extricated from Soviet occupation now, after the fact, we can boldly claim that the path chosen by the Estonian people has been one of the best. However, it must also be emphasized that "there are two sides to every coin" and something "good" in one sphere of life is accompanied by something "bad" in another.

Making a good choice presumes that the decision-makers are familiar with the landscape and know how to orient themselves within it. The most familiar model of political thought forces us to make decisions in a one-dimensional left–right arrangement. However, our actual physical and social environment is a three-dimensional space, with time creating a fourth dimension. In our everyday lives, we see that neither politicians nor voters are able to explain what differentiates left from right, or what a "third way" might mean in a one-dimensional environment. Political decisions are driven by emotions, words describing ideology are given definitions that suit the individual, and the making of the decisions that shape social existence is accompanied by endless bickering. The one-dimensional treatment of society is the best way to get people quarreling, because moving in one direction in this kind of space automatically means opposing all those moving in the opposite direction, and this, in turn, deprives us of the opportunity for rational discussion.

In the actual, multidimensional world, there are many more choices. In order to orient ourselves and to make successful decisions, we need a map that shows the landscape of various political thought in a way that allows its use to describe society's direction of movement. Such a "map" would allow political discussion to focus on ascertaining our current location, as well as foster discussion about the direction in which we want to move together, and which reforms should be implemented in our state. But since each "coin" has two sides, i.e. with each reform someone benefits and someone loses, it is indeed very hard to reach a compromise. To have a solution which ensures the sustainable development of society, we must go to the other side of "veil of ignorance" and take the "original position" as it was suggested by American philosopher John Rawls (1921–2002).

As the author of this book, my greatest passion has been and remains the wish to understand why different nations, civilizations and states are like they are, and why some have been more successful than others on the path they have chosen for themselves. I gleaned my first experiences thanks to my opportunity to participate in discussions (within the framework of IME [Economically Self-Sufficient Estonia]) involving the economic policy of the new state in the year 1987, as we felt that the Soviet Union would collapse and here was the opportunity to establish a new independent state. During this time, I realized with particular clarity that the determining factors of social development are, ultimately, nothing other than human emotions and needs, because neither states nor their politics exist without humans.

Because tax and fiscal policy were not taught to Estonians during the Soviet era, I decided first of all to educate myself in these topics. I acquired practical experience by working as an advisor for the Riigikogu (Estonian Parliament) Finance Committee and the Tallinn City Council, and the Financial Manager of the Keila City Government. From 1994 to 2015, I taught tax law and fiscal policy as well as fundamentals of economics and business to nearly ten thousand young people in Tallinn's universities and institutes of higher education. The worldwide economic and financial crisis of 1998 proved decisive, because during this time I began studying the history of fiscal policy and its influence on the development of states throughout human history. Basing my work on the monograph "Taxation and Budgeting in the Western World" published by Aaron Wildavsky and Carolyn Webber as the fruits of 18 years of research, I attempted, starting in 2005, to explain the principles of fiscal policy to my students, but only ten years later did

I develop an integral vision of how a fiscal system actually operates and how it shapes the progress and competitive abilities of a state.

Wishing to share my knowledge with others, I created a new study subject – the "History of Taxation and Budget Policies" – and decided to write my own fiscal policy textbook. But then I discovered that there is no such thing as independent fiscal policy – it is only a means for implementing economic interests and the ideology on which they are based. And so there arose the need to study various ideologies and systematize them to frame a logical picture or system of reference that could be used to describe fiscal policy. As the foundation of the reference system, I chose the concept of "Social Order" as used by Wildavsky and Webber. Building on their logic, I published the book *Three Social Orders and the Future of Estonia* in 2007. Unfortunately, their approach, which is based on three social orders (individualism/market, egalitarianism/sects, collectivism/hierarchies), turned out to be unusable (i.e. not logically explainable) in teaching. Instead, there evolved a two-dimensional approach with the axis values of "Equality" and "Freedom". Based on this, in my book *Political Choices Between Tyranny and A Welfare Society* (printed in Estonian) I described four social orders (cooperativism, individualism, elitarianism and bureaucratism) and all the more significant ideologies and forms of social order that various nations have implemented during the 6,000 years of known human history.

In this book, I will add another dimension – "Fraternity" – to the previous ones and, building upon this, I will describe a fifth social order ("Personalism") that is based on people who have developed personality, as well as a citizen society that some nations might attain in the twenty-first century or farther in the future, because it does not yet exist anywhere as the dominant form.

Here I would personally like to thank all who are prepared to exert themselves in order to learn about this very complex concept that differs so greatly from current social theory. I would be even more grateful to those who express the thoughts that come to them when reading and interpreting the material. The material presented in this book is not some final truth, but is, at best, an example of how to describe the history of humankind's social development in a way that everyone can understand. The same can be said about the vision of the future herein – in it is described only one possible vision (in addition to the many utopias and dystopias introduced through the years) of the trends in social organization and what they might be based upon in the future.

Paul Tammert

Tallinn, 2019.

INTRODUCTION

This book was born of a desire to understand the evolution of human society by looking at the history of various civilizations. What led some nations to success and others to annihilation? Is it possible to create a world in which everyone enjoys a good life?

As sad as it may be, a time of universal well-being will never be achieved in the material world that we know. In the jargon of physics, a situation in which all energy is evenly distributed throughout the universe is called "heat death". The main character in Johann Wolfgang von Goethe's *Faust* makes a deal with Satan, who promises to serve him until he says the words "Beautiful moment, do not pass away!". Both these examples imply that at the moment when differences and conflicts vanish and all needs are met, all movement and the ensuing progress will also cease, and material existence will lose its purpose and meaning.

Physical research has shown that the greatest amount of energy is released in an environment containing differences (areas of low and high pressure, heat and cold, acid and alkali etc), and where nothing prevents them from coming into contact with each other. The same can be said about human societies: inequality increases the developmental potential of the society. Problems do not arise until one party in a society or one species in a biosphere becomes dominant and begins hampering the progress of all the others. Studies of the history of planet Earth have repeatedly demonstrated that the "final victory" of one party is followed by a revolution or a qualitative developmental leap, after which the currently dominant party vanishes from the arena of history.

The next essential question is: "From what do human actions arise?" Evolution theorists claim that Life developed by chance – through the random union of atoms and molecules – and evolved without any kind of plan or purpose. But has anyone ever seen a beautiful house develop as a result of the random movement of a pile of rocks, a house that fully satisfies the needs of the people who wish to live there? We inevitably reach the conclusion that every new phenomenon arises from someone's need and from a thought serving the goal of satisfying that need. The construction of a house starts from an idea that takes shape as a blueprint, and goes on to take form as builders do their work to make it into a physical structure. Nothing comes into existence without a need, and nothing comes into existence without a plan to satisfy this need. Therefore, we can assume that the world and the creatures living in it have also been created by someone. Many call this creator God; in this case, Creator-God.

People are driven to act by their feelings and ideas, of which at least some arise from our materiate nature and the need to sustain our physical life. But the idea that emerges for the purpose of finding the best way to satisfy the physical body's next need is not materiate. And the environment of the senses, in which we assess the feasibility of the idea and the consequences thereof, is also not materiate. Even less materiate are the language, culture and legal order that unite people.

The approach to social theory presented in this book proceeds from the common person and the everyday feelings and ideas that arise primarily from the need to ensure daily subsistence. Since this has not changed over the millennia, the number of subsistence-ensuring behavior models has also remained the same. It is only humankind's ability to satisfy these needs that has increased and decreased. And since the number of subsistence-ensuring behavior models and the social orders that are shaped by them is small, we can use them as the foundation for our discussion of society and policy. Nations and states are distinguished from each other only by the relative proportion of the people supporting these social orders. And this in turn determines which policies can be implemented in said state and which cannot. This is exactly what this book and its subsequent addenda will attempt to explain to the reader.

THE STATE

WHAT IS THE STATE?

The state as an institution is an idea that enforces the rule of law within a specific territory; the vision of the organization of community life held by those people who participated in its shaping determines the essence of this idea. In material reality, the state is defined as the organization that unites the people living within a specific territory. It is created either through social compromise or by force, and its character is shaped either by laws or by the will of a ruler who applies coercive force to have his way.

States as virtual beings or legal persons recognize each other's existence and sovereignty (independence, freedom) through their representatives. Of course, this presumes that they are able to defend their territory and preserve its legal order, and do not endanger or harm other states, particularly neighboring ones. And although the state is, on the one hand, simply a subjective reality (existing in the minds of people), it is also an objective entity that coerces its population, by the application of various measures, to submit to the prescribed order. Yet, the state as an institution cannot be an entity that stands above the people and has its own will because, without the people's support, it ceases to exist. The "character" of a state changes as the world view and mentality of the generations who carry on the idea of the state change. And when the habit of living and acting according to common rules is lost, the state itself will vanish. It was Aristotle who claimed that the state is *"potentia"* (power, ability) as well as *"aktus"* (act, activity, behavior).

The idea of statehood arises from the principle that those public matters affecting all citizens of the Roman Republic (Lat. "res publica") must be organized in a way that satisfies all the citizens they affect. For this reason, the state that recognizes the freedom of its citizens is based on a social compromise that defines interpersonal relationships. In this regard, it would be correct to note that the concept of citizenship did not encompass all people in earlier times, and similarly today in some countries, because they were left behind, people who haven't real estate, women and immigrants – that is, those who did not pay taxes or participate in the defence of the land from the enemies.

The character of a state follows from the past experiences of its people and knowledge acquired from others; on this, they base their endeavors for shaping interpersonal relationships and the physical and social environment of the present as well as the future. The identity of the nation that makes up a state is inseparably bound to its legal order. Misunderstandings and conflicts arise between different states and their citizens because every one of them has its own legal order and vision of what interpersonal relationships should be like. Unfortunately, the ensuing cultural customs are not in the category of phenomena that can be ascertained with methods used for the study of the physical world and its phenomena. They can only be cognized indirectly, by analyzing people's behavior and interpreting the symbols and words that are being used.

In Indo-European languages, the concept of "state" is marked by derivations of the Latin word *"status"* (Eng. *"state,"* It. *"stato,"* Fr. *"état,"* Ger. *"Staat"*), which means the dominant order. The Russian word "Государство" comes from the old Russian word "государь", which means The Prince and refers to the oppression of the population. The Estonian word *"riik"* was probably loaned from the Old Swedish word *"rike"*, with a definition that includes supreme power of Swea people, their government, and monarchy. In Low German, the same word was used to refer to the empire. From 1920 to 1940, "Eesti Vaba Riik" (Estonian Free State) was used to designate the Republic of Estonia, apparently in an attempt to place special emphasis on the importance of freedom for the people who had brought it into being. The Finnish word *"valtio"* refers to the use of coercive force, while *"tasavalta"* bears the idea of equality or endeavors to equalize.

The concept of state sovereignty was born and solidified in France in the fifteenth and seventeenth centuries, during the period of the emergence of absolute monarchy and the territorial state. The French king declared himself the *"souverain"*, i.e. the independent bearer of the highest authority, having total power over all his subjects. Jurist and political philosopher Jean Bodin (1530–1596) agreed with and confirmed this concept, finding that every social order presumes the existence of an entity in whose hands rests supreme absolute power. In Bodin's opinion, this could be none other than a monarch, who, standing above all private interests and exercising the will of the people (*salus populi*), answers only to God.

Englishman Thomas Hobbes (1588–1679) discussed the egoistical nature of man, and concluded in his groundbreaking work *Leviathan* that conditions of absolute freedom would culminate with "war of all against all", and this, in turn, would bring about the annihilation of all society. Therefore, people must relinquish their freedom and submit to a person or organization that is able to enforce public order and ensure peaceful relations between people. Such an organization is the state, which coerces the people to abide by their agreements with the threat of enforcement and penal law.

The state is sovereign, i.e. it makes decisions based on its own free will and does not submit to orders from the outside. Sovereignty is ensured by a military force and security agencies that are able to protect the territory and its population from invasions by hostile foreign forces and restrain domestic crime. Well-defined state borders that are clearly marked in nature and are carefully guarded did not appear in political life until the start of the new era, along with the entrenchment of the concept of territorial states. Every state that wants to be sovereign and preserve its culture must have control over what is happening at its borders.

Every individual (person) and state has absolute sovereignty only if they are completely alone and not wishing to do or share anything with anyone else. As soon as an individual wants to trade goods, or the citizens of a state want to travel to a territory under the control of another state, they must enter into agreements on mutual rights and obligations, thereby limiting their right to sovereignty (the alternative would be to start a war and enforce one's own legal order within the disputed territory). By creating a common legal space, the member states of the European Union have voluntarily circumscribed their own sovereignty and recognized the legal order adopted by EU institutions ensuring free movement, trade, etc. However, since member states have reserved the right to leave the union if it no longer meets their needs, the union is called a confederation.

The state is sustainable if its citizens relate to it, accept it as their own, and recognize its sovereign power. This means, among other things, recognizing the right of the state, based upon the interests of society as a whole, to limit individual freedoms and regulate individual activities. The opposite of statehood is anarchy, which formally means that everyone has absolute freedom to do as they wish. But, in practice, it presumes that each person must independently ensure their own security and welfare and also have the ability to engage in peaceful cooperation with others in a way that will ensure the preservation of their life and property.

FORMS OF STATEHOOD

In everyday language, the word "state" is used to mean very different things and, through time, its essence has marked very different ideas. But all these scopes of meaning have in common the referral to a territory and the legal order recognized by its population. In everyday conversation, people typically use the word "state" to mean the bureaucratic organization that manages the state, i.e. the government. For example: "Why doesn't the state do anything to improve the circumstances of our pensioners?" or "Why doesn't the state raise teachers' salaries?", etc. Such questions should first be addressed to officials at the Ministry of Social Affairs or Education, and then to the government as a whole.

Specialization and the resulting market economy lay the foundation for the state as an institution. In the next section, we will look at the evolution of statehood through its various forms and see which social order supporters are dominant (the essence and characteristics of these social orders will be explained in subsequent chapters).

<u>Figure 1.</u> A figure illustrating the evolution of statehood by way of its various forms:

city-state > military state > territorial state > modern state > social state > citizen society.

The institution of the state arises from specialization, market economy and the need for the establishment of legal order and, as it steadily grows, it evolves from a city-state into new forms. By: P. Tammert.

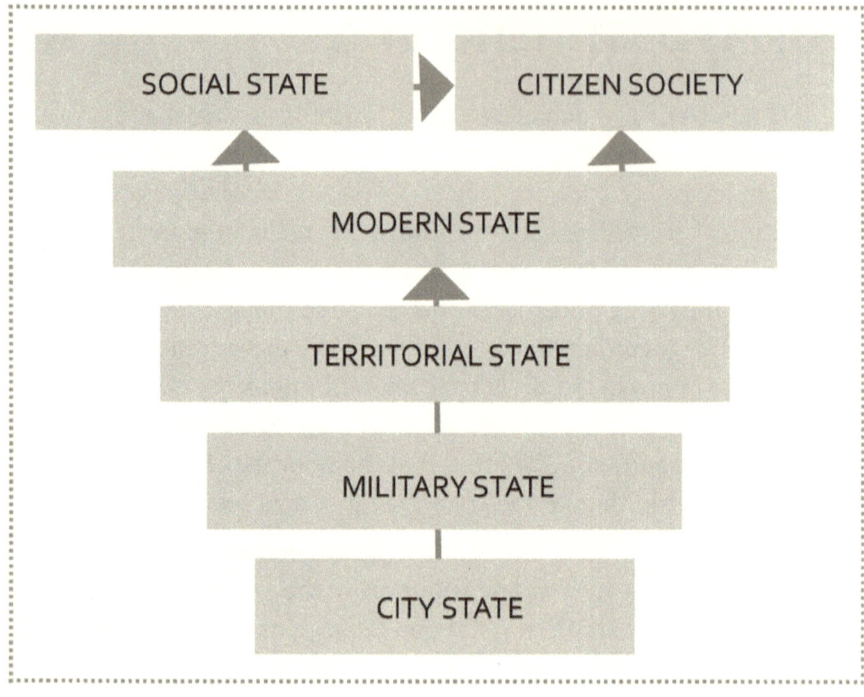

The City-State

Cities were born as a result of human specialization in one job and the need to exchange the fruits of one's labors. In turn, artisans and merchants lay the foundation for an individualistic social order, which has the market economy as its natural environment. Since specialization improves productivity and increases product quality, the city becomes a magnetic center where people throughout the region seek to exchange their goods for items that they need. The city becomes a regional hub to which all transportation routes flow. This is exactly what distinguishes a city from a village: its residents do not produce food themselves, but trade the goods they produce in exchange for food.

The city state can emerge from a single tribe, but its population will be formed from venturesome people from different tribes and races. But, the exchange of goods and services gives rise to disagreements about fair price, causing interpersonal conflicts. An impartial party is needed to resolve the conflict, giving rise to institutions of justice, the custom of recorded legislation, and specialization of officials, which all results in the creation of a bureaucratic organization. Thus, a precondition for the birth and development of urban culture is the ability of free people to organize themselves, horizontal specialization, and fair-exchange transactions in a market economy.

The characteristic of a city-state is the legal order that is enforced in the public space where goods are exchanged and which is protected by the city. The oldest cities are Jericho in the Middle East, which was established in the ninth millennium B.C., and Mehrgarh on the territory of today's Pakistan, from the eighth millennium B.C. From the latter developed the entire Indus Valley civilization, with large and well-planned cities, public buildings and enormous harbor facilities. Because no written documentation of these cities has been found, we know nothing of their legal and administrative systems that formed the foundation of their statehood. In contrast, the existence of the Sumerian temple culture and the administrative performance of the cities founded and administered there is recorded in millions of documents preserved on clay tablets, as well as other written materials. The most noteworthy characteristic of both the Indus and Sumerian cities is the size of their populations, which was 65,000 residents in the city of Ur (about 1% of the Earth's population in the fourth millennium B.C.), 80,000 residents in the cities of Mohenjo-daro and Uruk (third millennium B.C.) and 200,000 residents in Babylon (second and first millennia B.C.).

Most of the documents preserved from the cities of Mesopotamia are sale–purchase contracts between independently acting persons, as well as court judgments and all other kinds of administrative documents that archive important interpersonal events and the knowledge gathered during such activities. The oldest recorded legal principles are from Sumerian cities and are remarkably humane for the guilty party: a crime committed against another person was usually punished by a demand of monetary compensation or slave servitude that was annulled no later than the seventh year. All this allows us to presume that the dominant system was a market economy, which is characteristic of individualistic social order, in combination with various forms of temple bureaucracy.

The city-state model spread from the Middle East to Greece and from there to Italy, where it persisted for several millennia. After the fall of the Roman state, this model of statehood was carried on by the Italian trade cities, of which the largest – the Republic of Venice (Serenìsima Repùblica Vèneta) – endured until 1797 and, during its heyday, controlled half the waters of the Mediterranean. In today's world, this form of statehood is most clearly represented by the Republic of Singapore.

The Military State

Paving the way for the birth of a military state is a new vertical specialization seeking to redistribute the working population's income and property and consolidate the capital they need for their everyday subsistence (land, natural resources, money) into the hands of those who are directing this process. A variety of different tactics are implemented to achieve this goal, starting with civil wrong, amplified with the use of psychological pressure or manipulation, and culminating with the threat of direct force or even slaughter.

The concept of militarism is derived from the Latin word "*miles*" ('soldier') and its extension "-itia", which indicates action, condition or quality. In this combined form, the Latin word "*militia*" denotes military service. During the Roman Kingdom and Republic, it denoted the social service obligation of landowners and free citizens to protect their property and their freedom. The Latin word is "*malev*", which denotes a non-professional national defense force. In later times, the word *militia* has been used to refer to organized paramilitary associations of greatly varying forms. During the period of Anglo-Saxon domination of the British Isles (450–1065), it referred to adult men who were obligated to keep order in their land and defend it against foreign invaders. The word was used with the same meaning in England's American colonies. In Switzerland today, it denotes the reserve force of persons having previously served in the military and civilian residents that will be called into service with the outbreak of war. Its counterpart in Estonia is the Defense League. In developing countries torn apart by conflicts (i.e. "failed states"), it is the name currently used to refer to private armies. In the Soviet Union, until 2012 in Russia and until 2015 in Ukraine, police force responsible for domestic security bore the name "*militsiya*".

In the creation of a military state, one tribe or nation and its noteworthy leader have always played a decisive role; at this leader's call and under his leadership, they wage war against other countries and nations. Military states encompass a large territory populated by nations having different languages and cultures, and including cities with a distinctive legal order. With organized terror and military campaigns, the warriors annex ever more territory along with the component villages and cities, subjugating them to one ruler. The goal of a military state was and is to collect additional income with which to cover the subsistence expenses of the ruling elite and the warriors who safeguard their power.

Factors fostering the birth of a military state are people who fail to engage in cooperation, who value life more than freedom, and who fail to organize themselves in defense of the land that has provided them with freedom. The conquest of large cities by small groups of warriors (e.g. the Sumerian city of Uruk, population 80,000, was conquered by an army of Semites numbering about 5,000) has always been aided by large merchants whose business was hurt by the trade tariffs imposed by city-states.

A military state is born from the strength of warriors, and the resulting regime, founded on injustice, as well as the privileges of the ruling elite, are able to endure only with the support of continued coercive power. As injustice grows and restrictions on individual freedoms increase, the effective and innovative manufacturing activity that was characteristic of the previous individualistic city-state diminishes with growing speed, lessening the military state's ability to compete.

The military state means, generally, a permanent state of war. However, as hostilities continue, the number of tribal warriors decreases and the proportion of people who have laid the foundation for the militaristic lifestyle within the population diminishes. At the same time, capital is consolidated into the hands of a few successful individuals; most of the population becomes poorer, and injustice grows.

As a result of wealth redistribution, the original militia – a poorly armed military force comprising regular people – is replaced by a new type of military made up of the noble class with better armaments and sufficient means with which to continue honing their battle skills. In ancient societies, this meant the transition to horse-drawn war carts; in the early Middle Ages, to heavily armed knights on horseback.

As the locally ruling warlords-maintained order, dispensed justice and collected taxes, this wealth awakened temptation to use the accrued funds in their own interests. After building impressive fortresses for themselves and forming suitable military units from the people in their food chain, the boldest declared themselves to be independent of the supreme ruler, and passed on the position they had achieved to their descendants. In this manner, large empires shattered into small principalities with rulers whose main occupation was fighting with their neighbors and hatching plots to cause conflicts between other rulers as well as the more powerful interest groups in their own state.

A characteristic of the military state is a multicultural society. It is typically a territory brought under the power of one ruler; it is populated by tribes or nations speaking different languages, practicing different customs, worshiping different gods, and having different cultures of justice. The rulers of a military state are only interested in tax revenues and the availability of military recruits; in more primitive states, the availability of slave labor as well. The rulers offer nothing in return except protection from other forces who might want to tax these nations or steal their property.

It is notable that the cities of true military states in ancient times and the Middle Ages generally had a population of fewer than 5,000, and never more than 10,000. This was due to a way of life based predominantly on natural economics, which offered no other opportunities for subsistence. With the death of long-distance trade, the artisans' market became limited to the needs of the local ruler and his warriors, while the purchasing power of the local agricultural population remained modest. Only when the ruler stopped constantly traveling through his domains and established a permanent residence together with his court did a city's population grow to more than 5,000.

The activity of a military state is limited to collecting tributes and maintaining the established order. No contributions are made for the advancement of society and the public space, unless one counts the creation of associations needed for waging war. The warlords themselves engaged in collecting tributes. However, riding to each site once or twice a year to demand tributes was a dangerous activity, because not all tribes agreed with the obligations that were imposed on them. Collection of tributes became particularly dangerous when those imposing the taxes became greedy and started demanding more than the conquered populations were willing to pay. In circumstances where taxpayers must choose whether to starve to death or lose their lives fighting for freedom, many preferred the latter.

Ancient wisdom claims that "the power of a warlord ruler is limited to the territory that can be reached in one day by horseback". The invention of new means of transportation and the establishment of roads enlarged this territory, but the principle remained the same. If the ruler of a military state wanted to manage what was happening in a large territory, he was forced to share his power with other warlords or delegate power to local tribal leaders, also ensuring their obedience by taking their children hostage, i.e. to "school at court". The purpose of such schools was to groom the next generation's ruling elite by educating the ruler's own descendants and the children of tribal leaders together, thereby strengthening cooperation.

In the cities that had preserved freedom of trade, the obligation to collect taxes and keep order was delegated to city councils generally dominated by the large merchants. Because these merchants needed safe trade routes, they willingly cooperated with the warriors.

As the warriors succeeded in securing their power and vanquishing the conquered lands, they lost their desire to conquer, giving rise to the development of the manor culture. This became evident with the change of tax obligations: the obligation to pay individual ground rent now replaced the village community- or tribe-based tributes required up to this point. However, since the daily paperwork required for registering taxable persons and recording payment of their tax obligations did not suit the disposition of the warriors-turned-landlords, they had to include literate officials in their governing process. And the more these officials dealt with financial management, the more influential they became.

The military state model materialized, according to known information, for the first time in Northern Africa, where the climate changes (turning the fertile savannahs of the Sahara into desert) that began in the fourth millennium B.C. brought about migrations and a brutal struggle for survival. After centuries of massacres, the Kingdom of Ancient Egypt was established on the banks of the Nile to last from 2686 to 2181 B.C. This was followed by the Akkadian Empire (2334–2154 B.C.) that united extensive areas of Mesopotamia with many local towns (on the territory of today's Iraq, Iran and Syria). After the disappearance of the Sumerian city-states, the Assyrians – a people who initially gained notoriety with usury and slave trade – emerged as the dominant military force in Mesopotamia. A succession of invading nomadic tribes succeeded only in temporarily swaying their plenipotentiary power.

During the nearly 4,000 years following this period, the military state was the dominant form of statehood on our planet. The rulers of the military states competed with each other only with regard to the number of their subjugated tribute payers and the size of their territory. They sought to conquer not only the territories of other military states, but also tribes and village communities with a communitarian and natural-economy way of life.

The Territorial State

The warming climate of the Middle Ages (tenth to twelfth centuries) and the subsequent increase in the quantity of food gave rise to the rapid growth of Europe's population. The need for new living space increased the demand for artisans' products. This, in turn, lay the foundation for the rebirth of cities and the growing wealth of the bourgeoisie. Steadily growing demand stimulated trade, necessitating secure trade routes. The increasing wealth of the bourgeoisie as a source of tax revenue aroused the interest of the kings; however, receipt of these revenues presumed the establishment of secure trade routes that must also be protected. This, in turn, presumed the subjugation of sovereign liege lords and the annulment of their demands for customs duties.

To break the will of those nobles who had achieved sovereignty, the founders of territorial states used their most influential argument – gunpowder. The bullets that penetrated the armor of the noble knights and the shells that shattered the fortress walls of the liege lords also subverted their attempts to maintain sovereignty. Under pressure from the increased risk of death and the growth of economic interests, these nobles refused to participate in the brutal (i.e. very probably fatal) battles, and were prepared to pay a fee (scutage) in lieu of going to fight. With the money they thus received, the kings of Europe hired mercenaries, using these forces to subjugate new strategic territories and secure power over trade routes.

The territorial state, like the earlier military state, unifies vast territories under the rule of one sovereign. However, in contrast to the previous system, its goal is the creation of an integral living and economic space.

A characteristic of the territorial state is an integral legal order that is introduced and kept centralized by a secular bureaucracy, i.e. officials whose duty it is to protect the prevailing organization of power, public order and private property. Integral legal order presumes that the laws upon which it is based are recorded and available to every person living on that territory, allowing each individual to read them and act accordingly. This, in turn, presumes that every citizen of the territorial state can read and understand what the law says. The administrative capacity of the bureaucracy depends on the degree to which people understand the recorded order and are willing to take it into consideration.

The territorial state is a nation-state. The German philosopher Johann Gottfried von Herder (1744–1803) was one of the first to describe the relationship between language and thought, and thus also the comprehension of legal order. He claimed that not only every person, but also every nation, creates "their own world" based upon the history, common culture and peculiarities of that nation's language, influenced by the dominant religion. Herder pointed out the absolute uniqueness of living and historical national culture, formulated the principles of translation theory, and applied them successfully. He felt that since every culture is unique, the bearers of any one culture have no right to force their own culture onto representatives of another culture.

The subsistence and sustainability of a territorial state is affected by its size. The smaller the number of people maintaining nationhood or the smaller its linguistic space, the greater is the proportion of available resources that must be used to maintain the state as an institution and to enforce its legal order. Here we must remember that orthodox Christianity, based upon revelations and the writings of the Bible, is one factor uniting the European nations and their cultures. The translation of the Bible and other religious texts lay the foundation for the written language of many nations. The written language of today's Western European nations developed with the written records of Roman Catholic missions and legal order; the Slavic nations got their written language from the Byzantine Greek Catholic Church mission (ninth century Cyrillic), and the rest of the Eastern European nations from the mission work of the Lutheran Church. After the Lutheran Reformation, the state separated from the church, after which the secular government of the territorial state took on the burden of enforcing the legal order as well as paying the expenses of education. A nation that cannot or will not bear the costs incurred from maintaining its culture will lose its right to a separate existence and a territorial state.

Linguistic and cultural conflict is most bitter during the period in which the territorial state is forming. It arises between the nation wishing to create a territorial state that is as big as possible (more powerful thanks to the scale effect) and the rest of the tribes who would like to preserve their language and culture. If the tribal chiefs hold great influence over their people and are not willing to relinquish their plenipotentiary power, they deepen the cultural conflict until it expands into a full-scale civil war. This can be quieted only by an even greater external threat – one provided by a foreign enemy. For this reason, a wave of wars accompanies the development of territorial states. In wartime, domestic terror directed at minority nationalities is neglected or actually considered to be essential. In his book *The Invention of Peace*, British military historian Michael Howard (born 1922) aptly noted that a strong territorial state arises from blood sacrifice that brings the people fighting for their freedom (read: tribes speaking different languages and dialects) together as one nation.

Advancement of a territorial state is endangered and weakened above all by the demand for multiculturalism. In everyday life as well as in market-economy processes, recurring conflicts arise between people who speak different languages and follow different customs, culture and religion, because their understanding of behavioral rules, what is right, and what is just, are different. Cultural discord is exactly what is tearing apart the territorial states of Europe (Belgium, Spain, Italy, the Balkan states), Asia (especially the Mideast), Africa and America today. The discord manifests itself first in the economic sphere, growing into ethnic and religious clashes that damage the state's sustainability and finally even its existence. When the members of an intolerant culture, at the outbreak of violence, flee *en masse* to another state to continue their former way of life, justifying it with the idea of multiculturalism, these ethnic conflicts spread from one state to another.

Intercultural conflict becomes unresolvable if, within the territorial state, a region has emerged in which the population with different culture is dominant and does not wish to abide by the way of life that has been established by the indigenous population.

A solution based on capital, i.e. the right of land ownership prescribes, in this situation, that the resistance of the protesting population must be suppressed, by force if necessary and, if this is unsuccessful, these people should be deported or physically destroyed. As such, the capitalist solution would mean great human and material losses in a brief but successful war, or the emergence of a long-term conflict zone that continues to consume society's resources and impedes the economic progress of the entire state. Such a long-term conflict can end only with the indigenous population's loss of the conflicted territory and, in the worst case, with the loss of the entire state or nation, if the revolting residents cannot be subjugated to authority, and if other states start helping them with weapons and other necessary supplies. It is exactly these kinds of developments that we are seeing in the early 21st century in Georgia, Ukraine and Syria.

The humanistic solution is based on the people's right to self-determination. To prevent the spread of the conflict, the territory in question must be isolated, a new national border reinforced, and the area must be separated from the rest of the territory. Then, a popular vote must be held in the rebel region. If the rebels lose, they must submit to the will of the majority or leave to settle in a cultural space they find more appropriate. If they win, the following options arise.

- The winners of the vote form a Swiss-style autonomous self-government (federative system of government) and they have the right to decide how they will organize their life on this territory and to cover the costs thereof. During further negotiations, agreements will be made regarding which nationwide laws and obligations they will continue to recognize and which they will not, and how they will manage reciprocal tax and budget transfers.
- A new sovereign state is proclaimed that takes full responsibility for its own subsistence, and all reciprocal rights and obligations are abolished.
- They join a (neighboring) state to whose cultural space the population wishes to belong. In this case, the other state takes on the responsibility for what occurs in this territory and for the subsistence of the people living there. Disagreements on property rights are resolved through negotiation and payment of compensation.

The advantage of the humanistic solution is that it removes the ability of third parties to disrupt the future existence of the society and development of the state that lost the territory.

The evolution of the territorial state. The English laid the foundation for the development of their territorial state in 1215, when landlords forced King John I, imposer of excessive taxes, to sign the Magna Carta ("the Great Charter of the Liberties"). Among other things, landlords relinquished their right to collect local customs fees, but lay the foundation for the enforcement of an integral legal order and the institution of secular courts for the whole country. It was from this that the secular bureaucracy and parliament evolved. Under this legal order, the landlords had the right to remove the king from power if he failed to follow the letter of the law! This right was exercised by the members of the English Parliament when they dethroned and executed King Charles I. The secular bureaucracy fully established its power during the Commonwealth of England between 1649 and 1660.

On the European continent, the territorial state model was first implemented by the kings who ruled Paris and its immediate environs (Île-de-France), fighting bitter battles with the English for the right of succession and, in doing so, laid the foundation of the idea of the French nation. During these and subsequent wars emerged the France that exists in its current borders.

In the German-language cultural space, it was the Prussian rulers who set about establishing a territorial state, with the birth of Prussia after the fall of the German State of the Teutonic Order (1562). In the circumstances of an identity crisis, they adopted the Protestant religion and extended an invitation to all those people in other territories who were being persecuted because of their faith. The Protestant Reformation freed the individual from the total authority of the Church, and the introduction of literacy education expanded the freedom of the population even more. All this enhanced the progress of Prussian society, sciences and economy, and created the opportunity for establishment of a new kind of state ruled by law, administered by a centrally managed, hierarchically organized military bureaucracy. There was a popular saying at the time: "The Prussian Army has its own state." At any rate, during the time of its creation, it was the poorest and weakest of all the German principalities (in the Middle Ages, there were 356) but, thanks to the reforms, it became so powerful that it finally brought together most of these principalities to form a united Germany.

The concept of the territorial state was officially recognized in 1648 with the Peace Treaty of Westphalia, which ended the religious wars that had lasted for nearly a century. The treaty also recognized the right of Holland (Republic of the United Netherlands) and the Swiss Confederation to form their own state (without a royal ruler), establish their own military force, and collect taxes through a bureaucratic organization representing the government. The Montevideo Convention of 1933 stipulated that the attributes of a state are: a defined territory, a permanent population, and an institution enforcing public legal order (the government) that is able to maintain order on its territory and communicate with representatives of other states.

The Modern State

Territorial states with rulers who allowed the people's enterprising spirit and market economy to develop freely were responsible for the emergence of the industrial revolution in their land. An integral and secure legal system encouraged the owners of capital to make investments that might turn a profit only after decades. The productivity that grew, thanks to economic progress and the increase in specialization, also provided ever-increasing revenues for the government, which was now able to establish universal military conscription and assemble its own regular army. And this was an opportunity that the autocrats could not waste.

A regular army needed standardized mass production. This boosted the development of weaponry and technology and brought into use new means of transportation that enabled the transport of large numbers of troops over great distances. With the support of a well-trained and well-organized military, it was possible to continue expanding the domain of the territorial state and colonizing new territories and nations. The fact that the government was the largest and best customer of the large industrial companies paved the way for cooperation, or even an alliance, between big business and the bureaucratic organization.

However, acquiring new weaponry, transporting troops from one place to another, and engaging in direct warfare presumed ever greater spending for the construction of roads and infrastructure. Maintaining a regular army increased certain fixed costs within the national budget. Paltry wages, miserable living conditions, and attempts to increase the taxpayers' tax burden without listening to their opinions gave rise to tax rebellions and lay the groundwork for a wave of revolutions.

Here we should once again remember that the territorial state grew out of a military state ruled by the landowning capitalist elite. During the Industrial Revolution, they were joined in the territorial states by moneyed capitalists. Taking this into consideration, there is logic in the claim of Friedrich Engels, who said "the state bureaucracy is the instrument of the economically dominant class for the subjugation and exploitation of the oppressed classes". The nineteenth-century French anarchist Pierre-Joseph Proudhon articulated the idea of bureaucracy-free society, and in his manifesto *The General Idea of the Revolution in the Nineteenth Century* (1851), he brought forth the following ideas.

Democratization of the modern state. The wave of revolutions and wars that swept across Europe in the nineteenth century removed from authority the incompetent hereditary elite, whose members had either purchased or inherited their high office from their parents. They were replaced by educated people from the ever more powerful bourgeoisie who, in order to be granted the position, had to demonstrate their competence in the competitive market economy or personally demonstrate their submission to the regime. Royal power was replaced with a democratic system of government, separating those officials who organized governmental management and those wielding executive power from political officials who were elected to their posts and fulfilled a legislative role. This opened the door for new developments.

Characteristics of the modern state are, in an integral cultural environment and secure legal system, accelerated economic development, a highly developed infrastructure, and a market-economy environment that offers individuals new opportunities for self-realization. The opportunity to earn income and reap personal benefits from the fruits of one's labor opened the way for human creativity, and this in turn promoted the development of technology, increased labor productivity and enhanced social well-being.

The development of the modern state was supported by the enlightenment movement that began with the recognition of materialistic causality (relationship between cause and effect), separation of church and state, secular reform of the education system, dismantling of the guild order, and land reform. The latter process abolished the exclusive right of the hereditary elite to own land as capital. These steps were unavoidable if market-economy freedoms were to emerge. Raising the population's educational level and ensuring the free development of trade enhanced innovation and technological progress. The implementation of new energy sources (steam, internal combustion engines, electricity) and the transition from work done by hand to work done by machines paved the way for the wave of industrial revolutions. The implementation of factory production lines, the increase in transportation capacity (canals, railroads, highways, airplanes) and the development of communication equipment (telegraph, telephone, internet) increased specialization that expanded to the international level and paved the way for the rise of a global economy.

The unprecedented growth of labor productivity and production volume brought an end to the elitarian struggle for existence (the so-called zero-sum game in which only existing wealth was redistributed), because the abundance of goods improved subsistence for all members of society. The expansion of transportation capacity and the development of food-preservation technologies (canning, cooling, freezing, etc.) ended famine. The birth and evolution of the stock exchange created an opportunity to trade in large quantities of goods; it soon expanded to include quantities of goods to be manufactured in the future (futures). The development of banking and the recognition of the right to collect interest on monetary loans enhanced the development of the financial economy, but also increased the speed of concentration of capital and the financial stratification of the population.

Progress within society and the economy accelerates when the ruler or government of a state recognizes and protects private property, promotes private enterprise, and leaves people the freedom to decide for themselves what they need to do to improve their lot. Naturally, this is accompanied by responsibility – responsibility for one's own subsistence as well as for the consequences of one's decisions that affect society as a whole. Market-economy individualism has brought about only three known bursts of innovation throughout human history: In the city-states of India and Sumeria in the third millennium B.C., in the Greek and Roman city-states at the end of the first millennium B.C., and the one that began in the Anglo-American cultural space at the beginning of the nineteenth century. Precisely those things and technologies that were invented during these eras (starting with the wheel and ending with the internet) lay the foundation for the development of the modern state and provided opportunities to significantly improve living conditions for all people. During these periods, social wealth and human well-being increased to an unprecedented degree, extending also to the poorest members of society.

The modern state's advancement ability and competitiveness depend directly on market freedom or, more precisely, the ability of participants in the market to acquire what they need from the market and to sell their own products and labor on the market. The greater the freedom of choice for the market participants, the fairer the prices of exchange transactions. However, the preservation of this freedom is no easy task, because there are always egotistical and greedy people who want to appropriate the fruits of others' labors and privatize public property. Thus, in a modern state, the state bureaucracy plays an important role in preserving market freedoms, because it is only bureaucratic officials who have an eye on society's public interests, who have the right to limit activity fueled by the greed of private business, which would be able to destroy the natural environment as well as the sustainability of the society. The educational system as well as implementation of legal and fiscal policy measures can prevent the emergence of developments that limit the freedoms of self-realization and economic progress; in extreme cases, even coercive force must be used.

Crisis in the modern state occurs with the strengthening of the capitalist mentality in the market economy. The birth of capitalized big businesses, which turns the person into an accessory of the machine and makes stock shares tradable on the public stock exchange, allows the making of ever greater investments into the economy. However, at the same time, this detaches the owners of capital from employees, and allows the owners to seek ever greater profit without remorse. In a free market-economy environment, manpower is one production input among many, and the selling price of the manpower is entirely up to the seller of the manpower.

Thanks to the right of private banks to freely emit money for loans and to demand high interest rates, a new type of financial oligarchy evolves, becoming a dominant force within the state. By manipulating political parties as well as dominant politicians and high government officials, oligarchs try to shape an environment that caters to their advantage, using several kinds of lobbying organization and clubs (Freemasons, Round Table, Rotary Club, etc.). Limiting market freedoms and thereby achieving a position of monopoly – that of ruling the market – is the most effective method of serving one's self-interests. Greater unfairness in market relations brings about faster redistribution of the created profits, and society becomes stratified.

When money is removed from circulation as profit, and the effects of living on income from property and investments expand, the sustainability of the economy is damaged. A credit-based economy that requires the payment of interest and the playing of the stock market with capital concentrated in the hands of the few – for the purpose of maximizing profit – bring about economic crises of global dimensions.

According to Oxfam International, the beginning of the twenty-first century is seeing the wealth of the ruling elite increase at an unprecedented rate. Expert assessments claim that, as early as 2016, 1% of the Earth's population owned more capital than the other 99% combined. The personal subsistence hardships that are affecting more and more people stir up jealousy and anger, which endangers the sustainability of the state as a whole and, ultimately, the property and lives of the ruling elite themselves. If the state's bureaucratic organization is unable to solve the problem and placate the anger, populist politicians enter the scene, devaluing the democratic form of government and provoking a spirit of revolt. This may give rise to revolutions or even civil war, which will thrust the state back into the status of a military state. An alternative to such developments is the creation of a social state.

The Social State

The intensification of egoism and greed, along with the prevalent injustice in market-economy relations, create a situation in which citizens lose the private property that is the foundation of their liberty. If the state bureaucracy is unable or unwilling to limit this greed and injustice, the people are left with the right to choose suicide or to submit to the arbitrary wishes of the owners of capital. If, however, a free person does not want to submit to the arbitrary will of others and euthanasia and suicide are prohibited, they are left with no other option but to steal what they need to live or to take it by force. And they have the legal right to do so, because the society that created the unjust economic environment offers no other solutions. In these circumstances, the capital-owning elite has two ways to preserve their lives and property. If the elite wants to continue living in the same way, it must establish residential zones protected by walls and protective barricades and hire bodyguards for the times they leave these zones. However, even this will not guarantee the preservation of life and property if the masses begin to stir.

Thus, in summary, better results can be achieved if the state bureaucracy is given greater power to limit capitalistic greed, and also reserves the right to redistribute some of the revenues earned by businesses in order to support the needy. In return for relieving the working population of responsibility for their own subsistence, the officials can require complete submission to the will of those who execute governmental power (not the state!). This results in the establishment of egalitarian policy (i.e. redistribution of profit) and the door is opened to the development of a social state.

The characteristics of a social state are the supremacy of the bureaucracy, policies promoting equalization and welfare, and the regular limiting of individual freedom of self-realization. The concept of a social state denotes a form of government in which the bureaucratic organization (professional politicians and officials) becomes an independent power and begins to define the lifestyle for the whole of society and all its members. The bureaucratic organization takes public responsibility for the subsistence of the population, with the goal of relieving the stresses caused by coping difficulties and the uneven distribution of wealth. In exchange for submission and voluntary adherence to the enacted order, people are given the right to demand a better life and periodically to elect persons who they feel will best help achieve these goals. Since bureaucracy's logic of action is based on standardization, regulation, enactment of dictates and laws, issuing of operating licenses, checking on the legality of people's activities, and punishing violators, this lays the foundation for the strengthening of the plenipotentiary power of the bureaucracy. Bureaucracy extends even into business, where each step must be documented, and each position must have working instructions and an assigned field of responsibility.

With the growing supremacy of the bureaucracy, the population begins to enjoy increasing equality of access to goods and services, but is subject to an increasing number of regulations dealing with how everyone should behave and think. Thanks to campaign promises, people start believing that they can ensure their subsistence by merely voting for the appropriate candidate. This quickly leads to the redistribution of profits earned by enterprise, legislative limitation of personal initiatives and freedom of activity and, in extreme cases, enactment of a universal planned economy. The latter means that the bureaucratic organization nationalizes private businesses and assigns professional officials who are personally not responsible for the cost-effectiveness of their activities to lead them.

The concept of the social state contains elements of the elitarian world view, according to which people are either leaders of great intellect or members of the ignorant masses. The role of the latter, among other things, is to work and guarantee the well-being of the former. At the same time, the human desire to experiment, to experience something new as a result, to learn, and to advance, is left by the wayside. Therefore, the sustainability of the social state depends directly on how much room it leaves for private property and an individualistic market economy.

Humankind has realized very differing forms of the social state in thought as well as practice. States that have preserved a relatively high degree of market-economy freedom and allowed cooperative enterprises to play a major role in the economy have successfully implemented the principle of equal freedom of consumption. Such states are Austria, the Nordic countries (Denmark, Sweden, Norway and Finland), Iceland and Canada. Also, the Netherlands, Switzerland and Germany have succeeded in finding a workable solution by combining the ideas of the modern state and the social state. The operational freedom of businesses is significantly more limited in France and Belgium, where state bureaucracy is clearly dominant.

The suppression of individual freedoms and the enactment of the plenipotentiary power of officials has been most extensively executed by Russia (Soviet Union), the People's Republic of China, North Korea, Cuba and other totalitarian states. However, the idea of planned economy has also been applied in earlier times, for instance in the final period of the Sumerian culture and the Roman Empire. They were not succeeded by states selecting a national socialist policy, states whose rulers attempted to improve the welfare of their own people by increasing the exploitation of others (Hitler's Germany, Mussolini's Italy, Spain, Portugal, etc.). The chosen tactic of Islam, which represents religious socialism, borne by religious leaders and judges combined in one person, is to involve the European welfare states by taking advantage of social services and spreading the ideology of multiculturalism.

The problem with bureaucracy is that the officials themselves produce nothing. They can only redistribute the services or products manufactured by enterprising people or the wealth greedily grabbed by capitalists. However, nationalized property and the sense of well-being it provides does not last long. This effect can be compared to a situation in which a violent gang takes a family's cow and butchers it to grill the meat. Everyone feels wonderful at the banquet but, afterwards, they have neither a cow nor its milk, which had up to now provided the family with a small but steady amount of subsistence, perhaps by selling cheese or butter. In this situation, the family is left with no option but to join the gang of thieves and seek a new victim.

Indeed, bureaucratic measures can make it possible to equalize the consumption of material goods, but redistribution of intellectual wealth is not possible. An egalitarianist fiscal and judicial policy robs people of stimuli for creativity and responsibility for their own subsistence. Along with this, the drive to make an effort, the desire to take risks, and the willingness to contribute to manufacturing efficiency are also lost. Decreasing production lessens the officials' ability to redistribute revenues and property. When officials no longer have anything to redistribute, the masses become restless, which lessens the officials' ability to keep the masses within the confines of legal order. To suppress the dissatisfied and the dissidents, the bureaucratic state apparatus must call on the military and use terror to eliminate anyone bold enough to express their dissatisfaction or think differently.

The developmental pitfall in this social order is the extension of democratic voting rights to those who do not themselves pay taxes. When the number of people receiving monetary support from state budget revenues exceeds the number of taxpayers, and the re-election of political officials becomes dependent on the votes of those receiving government support, the officials start making attractive promises to the masses during election campaigns. Once the persons dispensing populist promises achieve a great victory and the right to govern, they must start making good on their promises – for which the government lacks resources. Increasing dissatisfaction among the population means that a second such election victory will not be possible. In order to preserve their absolute power, they must subjugate the media and judicial powers to their own will or, even more effectively, arrange a coup and put an end to the democratic form of government.

An individualistic market economy and the enterpreneurs that drive it are like locomotives that pull the train, i.e. society, forward. If the locomotive is wrecked by a populist or authoritarian system of power, the train comes to a halt and society's ability to advance and compete is lost.

Crises in a social state are caused by various factors. Societies that were swept into ideological extremism and chose the path of total equality fell into crisis because people lost interest in working and earning income. Since, in this case, only existing revenue or property can be redistributed (zero-sum game), the support system that allows for the functioning of egalitarianism is lost. Well-being societies are haunted by the same problem, albeit in a milder form. One way or another, when the state bureaucracy no longer has anything to distribute, it loses the people's support as well as any reason they have to adhere to the social agreement that obligated them to submit to the government in exchange for guaranteed subsistence.

The population's growing dissatisfaction is also caused by the dissemination of materials describing and popularizing sexual minorities and the conducting of corresponding public events, all in the name of equal rights. Similar problems arise from the intensive promotion of multiculturalism and the glorification of ethnic minorities. The first of these only damages the birth rate of the nation (a problem in the case of negative population growth), but the other takes aim at the preservation of the predominant culture and the legal system upon which it is based. In both cases, the outcome is a loss of faith in the officials representing the government and an increase in the number of supporters of nationalist movements. The concepts of a territorial state and a multicultural society are congruent only if the administration of state matters is decentralized and decisions are made at as low a level of government as possible, as it is done, for instance, in Switzerland (principle of subsidiarity).

The Citizen Society

A citizen society can emerge either from a modern state with a peaceful, market-economy-based democratic social order, or by way of a severe social crisis in a social state whose autocrats are no longer able to fulfill their populist promises. Since the citizen society is based on people capable of independent thought and decision-making (i.e. non-manipulable), the number of personalities and their ability to cooperate play a determining role in the birth and development of a citizen society. This presumes the suppression of egoistical profit greed, and the spread of an altruistic (i.e. viewing society as a whole) way of thinking.

As long as a territorial state-style social order persists, the citizen society will be monocultural. This is due to the need for an integral legal system that establishes a secure living environment based upon one language as well as the population's common culture and world view (read: religion). Because self-interest-driven and power-hungry people – those who implement deception and force – can be restrained only by the imposition of a uniform, law-based legal system and the state's coercive force representing the public interests of society, a multicultural citizen society is not possible. If, however, freedom is threatened from the outside (i.e. by military states), society must support, in one form or another, a military force that is able to defend the territory and population of the territorial state against the demands of the aggressor.

The characteristics of the citizen society are a decentralized system of government, separation of powers, and a functioning democracy. To people who are capable of independent thinking, this offers broad opportunities to participate in the decision-making process that affects public space, personal life and well-being, and freedoms of self-realization. Democracy is functional only if it can eliminate the influence that power-crazed leaders as well as masses driven by egoistical self-interest (here we mean that segment of the population that receives more funds from the state budget than it pays into it) can wield on elections. Also, a state that wants to offer its citizens the freedom of self-realization and preserve sustainability in a constantly changing environment must eliminate any factors that impede development, and limit the influence of people who obstruct change (conservatives). Since the development of the individual as well as society is damaged most by those people who attempt to achieve supremacy and hold on to any privileges that might be endangered by reforms, a citizen society must prevent the development of a ruling and hereditary elite. Only when the numbers of egoistic people wishing to subjugate others diminish to a marginal amount, and it is possible to keep them in check by using public social pressure and boycotting relations with them, will there no longer be a need for the territorial state's coercive power and the integral legal system it has imposed.

The citizen society is based on people who organize their own lives and take responsibility for their own actions, those who do not need externally imposed laws, official supervision, or penal policies. In their stead, there will be social morality, internal ethics, and complete transparency in the making of social decisions as well as organization of economic activities. Transparency in the use of of family, business, local government as well as state budget resources will make deception and pursuit of self-interest impossible, or at least very difficult, and will lay the foundation for the development of human relationships based on trust.

Market-economy democracy, i.e. everyone's freedom of choice to select whose products they buy and at what price, enhances the positive and constructive development of society, and leaves the seekers of unfair profits without gain. When purchasing consumers start to consider the behavior of producers in the manufacturing process and its effect on the natural environment and the advancement of society, those greed-driven businesses that damage the environment and daily human subsistence will go out of existence.

In Summary

The duty of the state as an institution is the creation of a secure living environment through establishment of an integral legal system. Because every nation has a different concept of what is right and how people should behave, the legal systems of different states also differ markedly. The level of development of the people in these states and the power relationships within the social order they have created are also varied.

All the forms of statehood described above are represented in the world today, offering their populations very different physical and social environments and subsistence opportunities. The form of statehood in each state has been determined first and foremost by the mindset of the people in that nation and their willingness to make progress. Submissively-minded nations oriented only toward material subsistence have come to terms with life in the poverty and misery of a military state, in the name of preserving their earthly life. Those nations taking a chance and being willing to fight for their freedom, even to the death, have become masters of their fate and been given the opportunity to form their own territorial state, then developing into a modern state. Where a mentality of dependence is predominant, as well as the belief that someone else will work and toil without compensation for the well-being of those people who cannot be bothered to make an effort and have no desire to improve themselves, society will fall into the deceptive lap of social statehood.

The problem of modern and post-modern societies, ones that offer broad opportunities for self-realization, is a diminished birth rate. And the problem of well-being states with total democracy is mass immigration from developing countries with a high birth rate, where the ruling elite, in its greed, has robbed their population of normal opportunities for subsistence. However, since uneducated people lack the ability to integrate into a post-modern society, they start demanding changes in the local legal system in order to establish a physical and social environment that is comfortable for them, leaning upon the concept of multiculturalism and taking advantage of those politicians who promote humanism. This conflicts with the concept of a territorial state and encourages the spread of nationalist sentiments. Tension is also caused by the fact that post-modern states compete among themselves for self-realization-oriented and particularly progress-capable persons, because it is exactly these persons who will guarantee the sustainability of these societies and maintain their competitive edge.

To me, as the author of this book, it seems that any social order organized at the state level and based on material values has exhausted its developmental potential. However, a society can become a citizen society only as a whole and with initiative springing from the lowest grass-roots level, meaning with the voluntary cooperation of people who have achieved a certain level of personality development. The citizen society cannot be achieved by letting a state- or capital-ruling elite convey their population to that social order in a way that allows the people themselves to do nothing.

PRINCIPLES OF SOCIAL THEORY

THE PROBLEM OF ORIENTATION

Assume that you have gotten lost in an endless virgin forest. And now, try to explain to your rescuers where you are. The situation would be even more complicated if you were lost in a galactic sweep of stars in the open expanses of outer space.

In order to orient ourselves in space, describe our location and thus understand whether we are moving in the desired direction, we need a system of points or coordinates on which to base our orientation. For orientation in ancient times, man had to find objects that everyone could see and were simple to describe. Such an object might be a hill, a river, a town, a large tree in a virgin forest, or a seaside cliff. In olden times, sailors used the stellar constellations for orientation on the open seas. However, if the location of a person in danger is unknown, a search must be conducted before undertaking a rescue attempt, using up a great deal of resources and time, and the person needing help may never be found at all.

Today, location is ascertained by the Global Positioning System (GPS) that uses satellites located in geosynchronous orbit above Earth. There are 24 of them in all and, with their help, we can determine the location, direction of travel, and even the velocity of any object on the surface of the Earth (in a two-dimensional space) within a mere moment. If, when in danger, we can send out a cry for help that includes the co-ordinates of our location, help will arrive quickly. Therefore, it is extremely important for every person, community, and society, as well as every state to know where it is located and in which direction it is moving.

A One-Dimensional View of the World

Plato's Philosophy

People perceive the world around them with the help of their sensory organs, using the information they obtain to create a sensory image – that which they recognize as reality. The ancient Greek philosopher Plato (about 427–347 B.C.) described the limitations of human perception using the allegory of a cave:

We, humans, exist as if in a cave. We are chained to the wall of a cave, facing a blank wall, with our backs to the cave opening, which is separated from us by a wall. Behind the wall is an artificial light source that casts shadows on the wall before us of objects being carried back and forth behind the wall, such that only the objects stick up above the wall; the carriers of the objects remain hidden behind the wall and they cannot be seen on the shadows. Thus, we can only see the shadows of these objects on the wall. We do not see the objects themselves, we see only their shadows that are cast by the artificial light.

Therefore, we might claim that in this changing world, we perceive only the false images of actual things. And thus we live with the mistaken belief that we are seeing actual reality. And yet, the greatest reality lies outside the cave, in the pure sunlight that is so blinding to us who have lived in the cave that we are unable to open our eyes in this environment until we have received special training. The real objects that are located outside the cave are ideas. That which we perceive with our regular senses is too little and limited to understand these ideas.

Within the context of Plato's line of reasoning, I want to draw attention to one-dimensionality: the objects that are being carried back and forth in front of the artificial light source and above the wall are moving in one dimension – left and right. This is exactly the case with our current political discourse, which differentiates only left- and right-wing politics and their corresponding politicians.

But light is accompanied also by other interesting phenomena. A beam of light refracts through a prism to become beams of different wavelengths that we know as a rainbow. And although everyone talks about the seven colors of the rainbow, few can name them. This begs the question: do they actually see these colors? If not, why? Can they not name them because they really do not see them (physical defect), or because they do not recognize them (lack of skills), or because they lack the appropriate word for all of them (a problem of knowledge)? Or, when they talk of the seven colors of the rainbow, are they simply repeating what they have heard somewhere or learned in school, and not even talking about what they themselves are seeing?

Actually, the situation is even worse! The space around us is filled with all kinds of vibrations having various wavelengths and frequencies, amplitude and oscillation planes of infinite variety. Human beings can hear only those sound waves measuring between 1–10 meters and traveling in a "dense" environment, and see light waves between 380–760 nanometers. We also perceive the effect of infrared radiation on our skin as heat, and the effect of ultraviolet light as suntan. All the other waves between zero and infinity remain undetected by us, because our senses cannot perceive them. As with this, most of what is happening around us remains undetected by us.

If we proceed from the shadow model described by Plato, one could claim that we are looking at an image, but

- we do not see the real things because we don't know that they exist and they haven't yet the name;
- we see only the shadows of intellectual reality in substance, but do not comprehend the actual nature of what is casting the shadows (ideas);
- we do not comprehend the nature of what we see because we lack the necessary prior knowledge;
- we cannot talk about what we are seeing because we have not become aware of the existence of the spiritual source of the visible objects;
- we interpret the things we experience based upon our own world view.

Thus, people see the objects (or their shadows) that move before their eyes differently due to their genetic and sensory differences, and interpret the information based on their own understanding of the world. The latter can be compared to a light-refracting prism that separates the information obtained into its primitive components, which the consciousness reassembles according to personal world view. In short: People looking at the same thing or reading the same text perceive and interpret it in their own way and draw different conclusions from it. And so, we cannot understand why other people do not understand us and why they talk about the same things in an entirely different manner.

Current Political Concepts

The interpretation and imparting of accumulated knowledge presume simplification. A one-dimensional or linear left–right division was brought into use during the great revolutions of the nineteenth century to explain the political trends in the modern world. This division was based on the seating arrangement of the French National Assembly and the Frankfurt Parliament:

- On the right were seated the Royalists (the Conservatives) who thought that royal power was the best that could ever be, and that nothing needed changing in the organization of society;

- On the left were seated the Republicans (the Reformists) who wanted to change the world and establish a new and better system of government corresponding to the needs of the time, which would give people the right to a voice regarding the size of tax obligations imposed upon them, and would free human existence from the tutelage of the elite.

Such a linear division, on the one hand, introduced a greatly simplified description of politics that engaged everyone, even those who usually understood nothing; on the other hand, the description gave rise to confrontation and disputes. This worked to the advantage of the society-ruling elite, because it prevented the the masses from joining forces and engaging in co-ordinated action directed at curtailing the prevailing injustice.

With the overthrow of royal power and the hereditary elite, and the establishment of a republican system of government, the people achieved their desired goal and won (at least a limited) right to decide for themselves how great a tax burden they would bear and what would be done with this money. The achievement of this desired goal opened the way for the emergence of new reformists, while the republicans who had encouraged the reforms up to this time became the conservatives, i.e. a development-inhibiting force. The new reformists now demanded market-economy freedoms and came to be called liberals. When this goal also was achieved in the form of a modern state, and economic stratification deepened, it was the communists and socialists who took on the role of reformers, demanding intervention by the state bureaucracy, the creation of a social state, and the restoration of at least economic equality. As the totalitarian regime didn't satisfy many, the new reformers – Social Democrats – started to expand the electorate and create a welfare society with greater market freedom. Once that was done, the position of reformers was seized by radicals who started to demand the closing of factories and the return to an agrarian society (Greens), expansion of women's rights and abolition of sexual divisions (feminists), or the complete elimination of legal provisions based on sexual characteristics and removal of gender roles from the educational system (egalitarianists).

Today, all named political movements that have achieved their goal in a certain state can be called conservative, because they want to turn back the clock to their glory days, i.e. to stop the progress of the human spirit and of society as a whole. And all this only to satisfy their own egoistic desires (the thirst for profit or power)!

A Multidimensional Approach to Social Theory

In light of what has been presented above, we can only be amazed at why we – who live in a three-dimensional space, with time comprising the fourth dimension – continue to describe economic and political processes according the the most primitive, one-dimensional division.

The social theory presented in this book has grown out of the social order theory cultivated by Aaron Wildavsky and Carolyn Webber (University of California at Berkeley) in the second half of the twentieth century. Their work is summarized in the book entitled *A History of Taxation and Expenditure in the Western World*. Thoughts have been developed further by Michael Hechter

and Christine Horne, who published the university-level textbook
Theories of Social Order (Stanford University, 2003 and 2009). The
approach of Webber and Wildavsky focused on three social orders –
individualistic market economy, hierarchic collectivism and
egalitarian sectarianism – but in their textbook, Hechter and Horne
describe five phenomena that determine the nature of social order:
individuals, hierarchies, markets, groups and networks.

The approach presented here has emerged from active social
communications and studies, in the course of which the significant
has become distinct from the insignificant. By observing the
reactions of my discussion partners and students to Webber and
Wildavsky's explanations of social and political processes arising
from the model of three social orders, the flaws of this model have
become apparent. During lecturing, a new, two-dimensional
(freedom : equality) social theory took shape; its axes depict the
degree of freedom and equality in the society or form of statehood
being studied. The inner logic of this model allowed delineation of
four social orders that, after a long period of reflection and the
charting of their characteristics, I have named cooperativism,
individualism, elitarianism and bureaucratism.

Figure 2. The foundations of two-dimensional social theory are the
EQUALITY (horizontal) axis and the FREEDOM (vertical) axis. By: P.
Tammert.

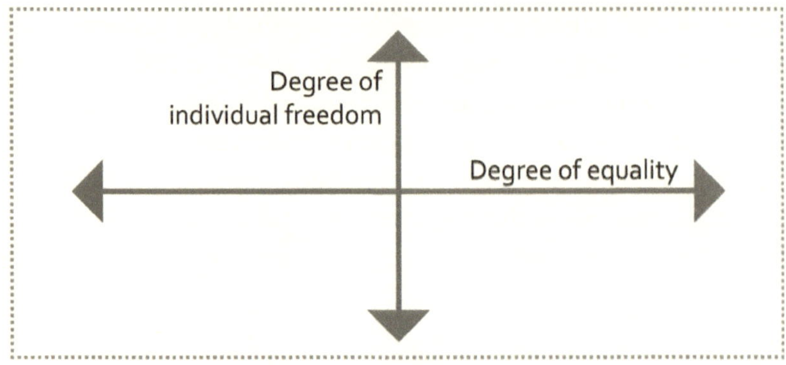

Now, for next I will describe a multidimensional model approach to social theory. If we tie in this model with the preceding part that discusses the development of statehood, I would like to note that the original cooperativist society does not create a state institution. It lays the foundation for the birth of a military state, which is upheld by elitarianism. The bearers of individualism play a determining role in the birth of the city-state and modern state, and bureaucratism achieves absolute sovereign power in the social state.

COORDINATE AXES

THE AXIS OF EQUALITY

The Meaning of the Concept of Equality

The concept of equality is connected to law or, more precisely, a legal system. A state that recognizes the equality of people must ensure every person's basic rights (the right to life, self-determination, inviolability of person, private life and private property). Significantly broader than these rights are human rights that were proclaimed worldwide by the United Nations (UN) in 1948 and include

- civil and political rights (originating from the natural law concept);
- economic, social, and cultural rights (these became rooted in the period of modern and social state development);
- rights of national self-determination and development (this topic emerged during the struggle for independence by developing countries in the 1960s and 1970s).

In real life, people have never been equal. The human genetic makeup gives rise to physical differences that are enhanced even more by the food consumed during the formative years and the knowledge acquired in childhood. A person's emotional world, value judgments and social orientation develop through mutual influences with the people and physical and social environment surrounding the person. Family customs, as well as the parents' knowledge, financial status and social position play a decisive role in the development of self-awareness. Chance plays a large role on a person's life path: forced and voluntary migration, some as a consequence of natural disasters and war, can tear people from their original environment and thrust them into very diverse situations in which some can cope and others not. The specialization of production and advancement of handicrafts and trade served to deepen inequality. Wars, deliberate exploitation of others, and the development of an elitarianistic class society entrenched and amplified human inequality even more strongly. Youth and age, sex, and many other factors provide bases for inequality, but also offer greatly varying opportunities for development and self-realization.

The ideal of equality is not found in nature; it is a human invention. The problem of equality did not arise in the primeval community, where a person's position was determined by membership in a family or tribe and its internal distribution of roles. It was unknown even in ancient and Midde-Ages class societies, because then a person was the property of another person – a talking tool! The issue of human equality did not become topical until the territorial state established a universal educational system to secure its legal order, and the enterpreneurs emerging in the Industrial Revolution began squeezing the last out of their wageworkers. To placate the dissatisfied and to reinforce the existing system – albeit in a somewhat covert way – the state bureaucracy introduced the idea of the redistribution of wealth (egalitariansim) and human equality.

The ideal of absolute equality is a Utopia created by the human mind that can never objectively be realized. Aspiring toward this goal would harm the progress of people, nations and states, destroying their competitiveness, because it directly opposes the concept of the competition that promotes development. Societies still trying to "jump over their own shadow" must choose whether to concentrate on offering equal opportunities for self-realization or to achieve equal right of consumption.

Equal right of consumption has always been championed by those who have been unsuccessful in everyday competition and have lost hope for improving their situation. We recognize that no one can live without food, clothing and shelter. And people can work only if they are paid enough for their labors to cover at least the expenses of the things that allow them to continue working (i.e. food, clothing, shelter, etc.). No one can work without compensation and only for charity, to support only others while ignoring one's own needs. And nowhere are there products that make themselves and that the government can distribute to the needy for free. Only with force can people be made to work for others without pay, in direct contradiction to the notion of equality.

The cause of poverty is typically a lack of knowledge caused by intellectual and physical laziness (except in military states where opportunities for acquisition of knowledge are lacking). But usually, the cause of human and national poverty has been the greed of employers who failed to pay their workers or paid them less than they needed to cover the expenses of things that allowed them to continue working. And if poverty is caused by the actions of rulers and employers, the charity of third parties can in no way improve the situation!

The spread of democracy in the social state granted suffrage to a large number of people who produced nothing themselves and failed to understand the relationship between cause and effect but were given a greater degree of political influence. Thanks to this, the topic of equal subsistence has become significant in popular elections and has given rise to a coalition of voters supported by government aid and politicians making populist promises. At the same time, these politicians usually know that the promises they make are impossible to fulfill, because nobody ever has the desire or ability to collect the huge tax revenues that would require.

In the remarks he gave at the 1984 Nobel Symposium, Swedish economist <u>Assar Lindbeck</u> (born 1930) stated:

> *It is often believed that conflicts over the distribution of income are likely to diminish when the distribution of income becomes more egalitarian, just like it is hoped that injustice and envy will diminish. ... Those who believe that the conflicts caused by distribution arise due to general inequality or differences in income, ... evidently assume that the drive to achieve equality will decrease as equality increases.*
>
> *For instance, the average voter believes that by moving toward greater equality, i.e. when the differences between small and moderate incomes become smaller, the conflicts caused by unequal distribution of profit will end. Unfortunately, this is in no way possible. We can also look at this from the opposite perspective.*
>
> *First, the conscious steps taken by public authorities to redistribute income give rise to political debates and conflicts about income redistribution more often than any other topic.*
>
> *Second, the willingness of individuals to increase their income by increasing their productivity decreases as tax rates increase. Furthermore — although this is rather more theoretical — people might be envious of only those whose income is slightly greater than their own, because this income is perceived within the limits of their own capabilities, not as compared to very wealthy individuals. The truth is that with the greater the equality of income distribution is achieved, the noisier the conflicts about the remaining inequality become, because more and more people have the opportunity to compare themselves with other people in similar circumstances.*

Thus, in a market-economy society, where the position achieved in the social hierarchy is defined by ability to consume (relative to one's neighbors and circle of acquaintances), it is never possible to fulfill the populist promise of "we'll guarantee consumption equality", because the more people get, the more they want.

The equal right of self-realization is connected to economics and the availability of resources that one needs to complete the period of one's childhood and education, and to enter the market economy and function within it. This includes eating quality food and living in a healthy and intellectually stimulating environment during childhood, acquiring knowledge and working skills during one's youth, and having equal opportunities for the acquisition of raw materials and the selling of one's products during adulthood. However, since all people are not alike, the outcome in a world with equal opportunities is inequality. Indeed, this could be called a natural inequality that never expands too much and undergoes constant change, because a person's working ability, skills and value judgments change during one's lifetime. For instance, a person who is very materialistic during their youth might later become a very spiritual individual who no longer cares for material wealth and prefers to work in a charitable capacity instead. Evolution in the opposite direction is also possible.

Equality of opportunities for self-realization presumes that all persons

- enjoy a similar status, regardless of their origins;
- have an equal right to a healthy life, education and self-fulfillment;
- have the equal right to express their thoughts, assemble, and participate in making the social decisions that affect their subsistence and well-being;

- have the right to have income from the fruits of their labor;
- have the right to use private property to serve their own needs and interests.

Divisions of the Axis of Equality between egoism and altruism

The horizontal axis of the social order model measures and describes the distribution of income and capital in society. Income does not appear by itself! It comes from the fruits of labor and grows when work is performed astutely and in an organized manner. When people leave part of the fruits of their labors unconsumed and prudently put it aside to ensure subsistence during a fruitless period, their independence grows. However, if a person obtains private possession of property that is necessary for subsistence, such as land, natural resources or money (i.e. capital), that person will become independent. As the capital owned by one person increases to become greater than what is necessary for the satisfaction of that person's own needs, it becomes a means of exercising power. By renting out land or lending capital, the owners of capital can satisfy their egoism and cause inequality to increase.

However, in addition to material capital, there exists social capital, which manifests itself in a feeling of solidarity within society (family, tribe, community or nation). If a person feels that he or she "belongs" in the society and its members trust each other, then economic activity becomes more effective, because the barriers protecting private interests (i.e. the question of what are my obligations and how much will others benefit) will disappear, as well as expensive legal battles over rights and obligations. The extent of social capital becomes most clearly apparent in crisis situations, when people either band together to protect the interests of their community or enterprise or flee the sinking ship like rats.

Figure 3. Trends on the axis of equality are most strongly influenced by human feelings and desires.

EGOISM, i.e. personal gain and greed, the desire to own more material capital and the drive to protect private property, dominates on the RIGHT side of the axis.

ALTRUISM dominates on the LEFT side of the axis. This concept includes the aspiration to ensure the sustainability of selfless charity as well as society as a whole, requiring social capital and common property. By: P. Tammert.

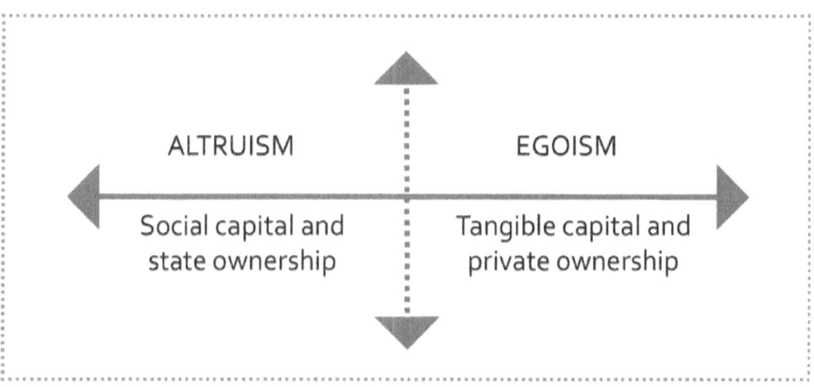

Equality is shaped in a society by two human emotions – egoism and altruism. The word "egoism" denotes a mental model based on self-interest, one that begets greed and avarice, i.e. the desire to own things or money (capital) in a quantity exceeding the person's own needs, and the desire to continue adding to possessions. The German-American philosopher Erich Fromm (1900–1980) described greed as a bottomless pit which exhausts people in their endless effort to satisfy their needs without ever reaching satisfaction. Generally, by greedily accumulating property, people try to relieve deep-seated feelings of inferiority, and to use those things (luxury-brand necessities, gold and precious stones, palaces, luxurious vehicles, etc.) to demonstrate wealth, thereby demonstrating their superiority to others. Greed harms the existence of people, the nation and the state when the greedy parties take away the property other people need for subsistence and uses it to strengthen their own position. Here it matters not whether these people are enterprising usurers or governing officials; they are distinguished only by the extent of the damage that their selfish activities cause.

The word "altruism" is typically used to denote selfless charity; doing good to others. Here, "good" can mean alleviating pain, improving subsistence, creating pleasure or happiness. Actually, the word "philanthropy" is a better fit for this context; the word is derived from the Greek "φιλανθρωπίc" ("person-loving"). That word is derived from the words "φίλος" ("caring for or feeding others out of love") and "άνθρωπος" ("human being or being human in the sense of humaneness"). The Ancient Greek playwright Aeschylus (525–456 B.C.) used the concept of philanthropy in one of his tragedies to mark the self-sacrificing behavior of Prometheus (Prometheus stole fire from the gods and gave it to humanity) for the good of humankind. As punishment for this deed, he was bound to a rock, where birds would feed on his liver. This symbolized the misery of a person in distress, caused by his inability to take care of himself, as well as the self-sacrificing act of a demigod that saved humanity from destruction. From this tragedy emerged the idea that people with the knowledge and means to help people in distress escape their misery, must use these resources to help their fellow man, even if they receive nothing in return. In this way, the word "philanthropy" came to mean charity, i.e. helping those in need, helping those who cannot ensure their own subsistence. Such activity presumes voluntariness and selflessness, and is often interpreted as an expression of self-sacrificing, altruistic love for one's fellow human beings.

It is likely that the people living together in ancient communities helped their needy companions as best they were able. But in a vertically specialized class society, charity became the privilege of the elite. Under the influence of the Catholic religion, philanthropy, with its meaning of selfless love and charity, was replaced by a new egoistic concept – soteriology, which focused on seeking salvation in order to save one's soul from the torments of hell in the afterlife. For the most part, this was the problem of the wealthy hereditary elite, profit-greedy merchants and usurious money-changers. To save their souls, they had to donate to charitable religious associations or finance the construction of institutions serving the public interests of society (church, cathedral, monastery, poorhouse, etc.) with the land and property they had amassed through deception.

In the waves of revolution sweeping nineteenth-century France and Germany, the original meaning of humanism, with emphasis on ethics and human relationships, once again came into use at the influence of the Hegelians, but mostly in the context of redistribution of wealth (egalitarianism). In contrast to religious humanism, it cast aside personal responsibility as well as charitable activity for the purpose of achieving salvation. The new, secular philanthropism emerged from the bureaucratic organization of the territorial state, and was focused on relieving the social tensions created by unequal distribution of wealth.

In the modern state, philanthropy has come to mean activities for the purpose of improving public well-being at the initiative of the wealthy. In everyday life, this is is manifested by one-time or regular donations and voluntary work. In his book

Lester's History of the United States, American sociologist <u>Lester Salamon</u> (1943) defines philanthropy as the voluntary giving of time or valuables (money, securities, things and other property) for the betterment of public well-being or their donation to a charitable organization.

Philanthropy becomes a problem in the bureaucratic social state where populism has caused an emphasis shift to human rights, with personal responsibility no longer a topic. This creates a situation in which people lose interest in exerting themselves in the name of self-realization, while the "do-gooders" encourage them to demand the same level of well-being and plentitude of possessions as their neighbors have. Because nobody is willing to work for the good of one's fellow man all the time, and without compensation, such a society ultimately becomes bankrupt and general chaos ensues.

In evolutionary biology, altruistic behavior is associated with self-sacrifice, for instance in the case of bees, who, by stinging an intruder, sacrifice their lives to protect their swarm. In human psychology, the model of altruistic behavior is described as a <u>meme</u> (model of behavior) that is adopted from parents or other influential people. Scientific studies have shown that the same part of the brain that is stimulated during eating and sex is activated during altruistic activity. Altruistic acts improve the sustainability and competitive edge of society or the state as a whole.

However, the concept of "altruism" also has another meaning that refers to the big picture thought process, i.e. placing the common interests (sustainability, perpetuation) of the family, community or nation above one's personal desires (but not needs). In this context, the word "altruism" acquires the meaning of *"paideia"* (Greek παιδεία), referring to the necessity of educating people and raising them to be citizens – something that is considered a truly altruistic act. In practice, this meant that "those in need should be given a rod and taught how to fish"! This kind of idea appears in Plato's *Euthypro* dialog (about 397 B.C.), in which Socrates tells of sharing his knowledge with listeners for free, calling it humanistic charity. Indeed, in Italy, the concept of altruism acquired the definition of free humanistic education. In the first century B.C., the Roman teacher of Latin <u>Aulus Gellius</u> (125–180 B.C.) noted the following in his *Attic Nights* (XV):

> *Those who have spoken Latin no longer give the word "humanitas" the meaning which it is commonly thought to have, namely, this word was once used to signify friendly relations and a spirit of cooperation between people that was signified in Greek with the word φιλανϑρωπία ("philanthropy") and precluded the exclusion of anyone. However, now the Greek word παιδεία has come into use as meaning ("education"), which we call "eruditionem institutionemque in bonas artes" or education and training in the liberal arts. It is now said that those who earnestly desire and seek after this knowledge are the most highly humanized. The desire to pursue this kind of knowledge and to put it into practice has been granted to man alone of all the animals, and for that reason it is termed "humanity".*

The issue of education became topical once again in twelfth- and thirteenth-century Italy with the discovery of numerous Ancient Greek and Roman manuscripts, the study of which brought about the rediscovery of a world view centered on the human being. Italian poet and scientist <u>Francesco Petrarca</u> (1304–1374) and writer <u>Giovanni Boccaccio</u> (1313–1375), enthused by the works of Roman philosopher, politician, orator and statesman <u>Marcus Tullius Cicero</u> (106–43 B.C.), were the first to introduce them to the world. Republic of Firenze jurist, writer and later chancellor <u>Coluccio Salutati</u> (1331–1406) purchased copies of more than 800 ancient manuscripts and assembled persons of noteworthy erudition around him, thereby establishing preconditions for the emergence of a new kind of secular educational institution. These schools focused on subjects that encompassed language, rhetoric, poesy and ethics, acquiring the common name of *"humanitati"*. Teachers of these subjects were called *"umanista"* ('humanists'). In contrast to God-centric theologians, they set humans at the center of the universe, together with their ability to change the world according to their own countenance and desires by using knowledge. This was as yet unheard of in a culture where a person's most important duty was thought to be the seeking of salvation and preparing to meet the world that awaited after death.

The European Renaissance (1350–1600) gave birth to a completely new spirit of the time (*Zeitgeist*). Into its center rose the curious human who would study the world without prejudice, amass knowledge, systematize it and pass it on by way of secular educational institutions. The way to Renaissance progress was paved by Firenze, Bologna, Venice and Rome. It spread northward from these cities, giving rise to the important centers of Bille and Nürnberg in Germany, Louvain in Belgium, Alcala de Henares in Spain, Krakow in Poland and, of course, Paris and London. The invention of the printing press in Germany by Johannes Gutenberg (1394–1406) and its rapid spread throughout Europe paved the way for a new wave of humanistic advancement that has been given the name of the Baroque Period (1600–1750), which in turn opened the way for the Age of Enlightenment (1700–1800). During the revolutions and world wars that followed, the chains of class society were broken, and a new, modern world emerged, founded on education.

Such a model of philanthropy presumes that the needy can clearly define their needs and present them publicly to their fellow citizens. The latter are obligated to determine how much it will cost to satisfy the request and how to cover the costs. Proceeding from the notion that life is granted to all persons for the purpose of engaging in self-realization and thus contributing to the development of one's own character, thereby also contributing to the sustainability of society, this also presumes that the recipient of aid will give society something in return. Thus, recipients of aid must come to an understanding with the providers of aid regarding the obligations they will assume to society and must fulfill these obligations. By refusing to take on obligations, they lose the moral right to ask for aid or sustenance.

The center of the axis of equality denotes the ever-changing state of natural inequality, meaning that each person's wealth depends on how much they have given of their physical and intellectual strength, and how strongly they have applied their willpower for the purpose of achieving their goals. Those who have not felt like exerting any physical or intellectual energy or applying any willpower to overcome obstacles are incapable of doing or understanding anything. They cannot orient themselves within the environment; they fail to see the cause of problems, and are unable to set goals to improve their subsistence. For exactly this reason, they are left without anything, but are quick to demand the reinstatement of "justice", which in their mind means equal right of consumption, while failing to take their failure to make contributions into account. But those who have given of their physical strength by engaging in hard manual labor or of their intellectual strength by amassing and applying knowledge have a score for their efforts: the size of their wealth.

THE AXIS OF FREEDOM

The Meaning of the Concept of Freedom

The concept of freedom is associated with motion. An object in the physical world moves freely in the absence of limitations or forces that direct or interfere with its movement. For humans, this means the right to freely choose one's place of employment, residence, and spouse, to procure necessary goods and services at a fair price, and to sell the fruits of one's labors wherever they command the best price.

In the intellectual world, freedom is associated with the emergence of self-awareness and personal development that becomes evident with self-realization. It is expressed by freedom of thought, speech, activity and free will, and becomes apparent when the people's behavior model changes. The need for self-realization emerges only in people who have achieved self-awareness, have the courage to express their will, and take risks in the real world by putting their knowledge to the test, while also being willing to accept the consequences of their actions.

It makes no sense to talk of self-realization if people lack the necessary resources to keep their physical body alive or if independent activity is not allowed. Assertive people who apply economic, legal or physical measures in the name of redistribution of property are the ones who cause hardships and limit the freedom of activity. In practice, this manifests itself as unfair economic transactions, threats of the torments of hell or prison, or use of personal force.

Going down the path to self-realization means changing one's current mode of behavior, which then inevitably impacts the subsistence and welfare of all other members of society, as well as the current state of society as a whole. This endangers or harms the position of those people who have asserted themselves in society, as well as their ability to manage capital. In this situation, one must choose whether to recognize the ideal of freedom, allow change, and go along with the process of change, or to bring an end to it, halt any progress, and strengthen one's own position of dominance.

In English, this latitude is known by two terms: "freedom" and "liberty". The first relates to free will and identity of self, including moral responsibility within society. In politics, the concept of "freedom" relates to state sovereignty and the right of people to assemble in the public space, assemble into organizations representing their personal interests, elect the representatives they find suitable, and express their opinion on topics that affect them personally. Thus, the word "freedom" denotes the ideal, the state of complete independence that disregards the rights of others and is not limited by factors in the material world.

The word "liberty" recognizes factors in the material world as well as the rights of other persons, thereby limiting a person's freedom of self-realization by its very nature. Thus, liberty exists within the frame of the person's world view, physical and social environment, social institutions, and state political order.

The concept of freedom/liberty stands opposite to the concept of determinism, which denies the existence of free will. The latter relates to the concept of assertiveness, whereby predestination may arise from a divine act of will, national necessity, or the interests of the owner of capital.

Divisions of the Axis of Freedom

The (vertical) axis of freedom measures the level of individual freedom in a society, i.e. what proportion of the people have the freedom of self-realization according to their own wishes. People can wish for anything ("freedom!") of their own free will. For example, they may want to fly away, but no matter how long they flap their arms, they cannot rise into the air like a bird. In order to realize an idea that forms the foundation of one's self-realization and to achieve the desired outcome, people must acquaint themselves the limits set by nature or society and find a way to overcome them (build an airplane). This, in turn, presumes knowledge and the ability to cooperate with others, because no one person has the knowledge and skills for everything. Therefore, people must take into account the demands arising from others' need for self-realization (the democratic decision process) – or assert themselves and subjugate others to their will.

A person is absolutely free only if living completely alone. However, a person living alone is able to accomplish very little. But living together with other people, in society, creates problems! What should one do when the goals of all parties are different – or even worse – opposite of each other? Solutions for such a situation might be:

- I will impose my will upon others, i.e. I am free to realize what I want, but others lose their freedom completely;
- They force their will upon me, and I lose my freedom completely;
- We enter into negotiations to find a compromise solution that satisfies us both. In the context of freedom, this means that both of us abandon some part of our initial goal. Thanks to a solution that partially satisfies the needs of both parties, and the voluntary partial

abandoning of one's goals, the subsistence of both parties is ensured and their opportunities for self-realization are improved.

The center section of the axis indicates people who lack the self-awareness or sufficient knowledge to express their opinion, or who lack the courage to stand up for their rights. In politics, these people are called the "political swamp" or "the silent masses".

Moving upward from the center of the axis, people enters the path of self-realization. They can protect their needs by participating in social discussions, democratic voting processes, and market-economy transactions to guarantee an outcome that changes society's behavior models. They can improve their well-being by undertaking something and implementing new approaches in economic activity. Thus, the line that extends above the axis of freedom can be described as a **lifestyle** in which people recognize each other's proprietary rights and freedom of self-realization, prevent deception, and ban any right to implement force. The will of the majority dominates here.

Moving downward below the axis of equality means taking the path of free <u>assertiveness</u>, which restricts the freedoms of other people, refuses to recognize their rights, and implements various methods of subjugating their will. Thus, the line extending below the axis of equality can be described as showing implementation of various **governmental cultures**. In this segment, the will of the minority dominates. However, the minority can force its will onto the majority only if it can manipulate the population's "public opinion" and make the government organization enforcing the legal order act in support of the minority's interests.

<u>*Figure 4*</u>. On the (vertical) axis of freedom, the desire for SELF-REALIZATION and the desire for SELF-ASSERTION (i.e. subjugating others to one's will) stand as opposites. By: P.Tammert.

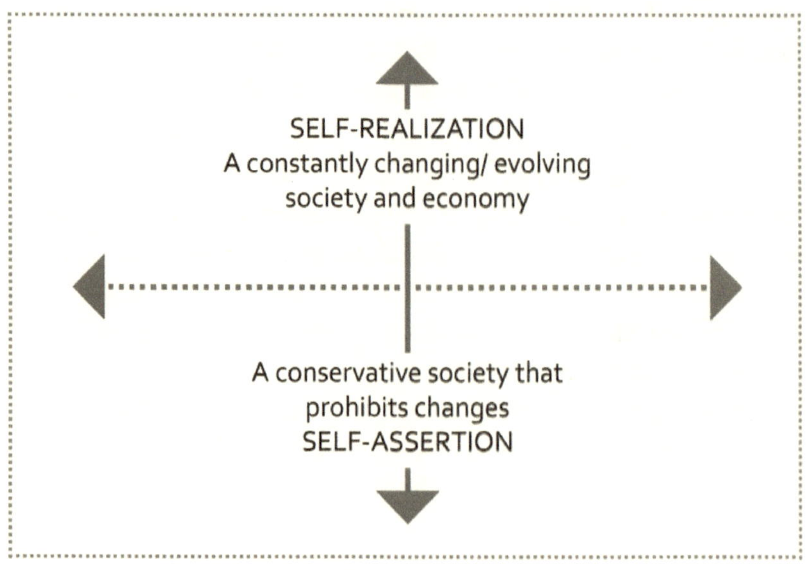

Social order

About the Concept

The modern states have created a world of very rapid technological advancement. The technology being used as well as the knowledge on which their usage is based are changing constantly. Increasing specialization and growth of productivity have given rise to unprecedented social well-being. Positivist philosophers of the Age of Enlightenment (Auguste Comte, Jean-Jacques Rousseau and others) articulated the concept of social development and began describing history as an ascending linear trajectory.

However, the consumption-based economic model has started to endanger humankind's existence. The Gaia hypothesis describes planet Earth as a living organism characterized by an integral system that can maintain its pre-determined parameters for a long time and respond to changes that endanger its existence. The topic of Earth as a conscious being was discussed by Peter Russell (born 1946) in his 1982 book *The Awakening Earth. The Global Brain*. Because the unfettered growth of the human population has begun to endanger the organism's survival, it is responding to the danger by temperature increases (fever) and movements of the earth's crust (earthquakes and volcanic activity).

The source of the problem is the ideology oriented toward development and growth which refuses to recognize that human nature remains unchanged. As always, humans continue to need food, clothing and shelter, and others of their own kind around them with whom to communicate and ensure mutual subsistence. And there exists only a limited number of opportunities to satisfy all these needs. The two-axis model offers only four models for mutual human relationships and assurance of subsistence. Let us call them four different <u>social orders</u>, to differentiate them from organization of society, which includes them all.

The English philosopher <u>Thomas Hobbes</u> (1588–1679) was the first to scientifically define "social order" in his work entitled *Leviathan*, which did not come into extensive use until the late nineteenth and early twentieth centuries, mainly because the contemporary social theoreticians were trying to find answers to the questions raised by Hobbes. Generally, the concept of social order was used then, as well as later, to refer to the rigid class society of the Middle Ages, with the Church playing the dominant role. Therefore, it is hardly surprising that the concept acquired a connotation of backwardness that a progress-focused culture was trying to forget.

American sociologists <u>Michael Hechter</u> and Christine Horne note the following in the foreword to their book *Theories of Social Order*:

> *During the turbulent days of the late 1960s, a concern with social order was often perceived as a barely disguised conservative apology for an ethically dubious status quo. Students' interest shifted to matters of social transformation. Now many of those same students constitute the senior faculty in sociology departments around the globe.*
>
> *The second source is intellectual. Sociologists of the postwar generation who were devoted to grand theory wrote much about how values and culture resolved the problem of social order. Because these concepts are inherently ambiguous, however, too little of this work had any recognizable empirical implications.*
>
> *But these are not good reasons to abandon a concern with social order. Although for some (Adorno 1976), grand theory's lack of empirical implications was taken as a badge of honor*

rather than a lacuna remaining to be filled, this was far from the mainstream view. As the emphasis on sound empirical research increased in sociology and the allied social sciences, many scholars and teachers found, and continue to find, precious little to admire in these highly abstract treatises. Further, dismissing social order as a concern of conservatives alone obscures the point that order is simply the flip side of conflict and change. A full explanation of social order requires an understanding of its transformation as well as its production.

No comparable intellectual rationale for sociological theory has ever superseded the problem of social order. Without social order, there can be no agriculture, no industry, no trade, no economic investment, no technological development, no justice, no art, no science, and no human advancement. Although it is frequently unacknowledged, the problem of social order underlies questions of central concern to sociologists in substantive areas as diverse as crime and deviance, social movements, organizations, politics, religion, international relations, and the family.

Four Social Orders

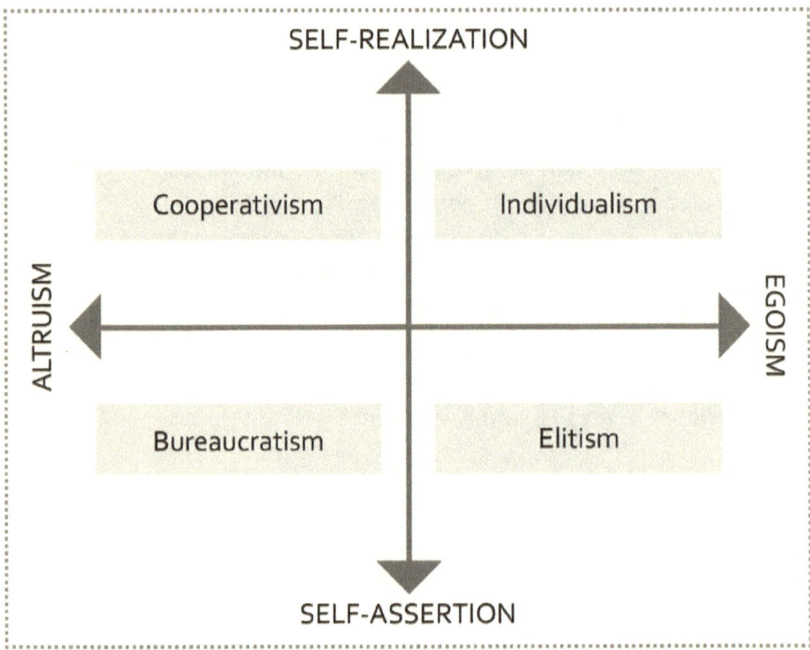

As a concept, the expression "social order" designates a type of human relationship implemented by humans to ensure their subsistence. Because humans, as social creatures, solve their problems in a community-based manner – i.e. within a society – the number of possible solutions is limited, and their form remains unchanged through time and space. Searching for suitable names for these standard forms, the following terms made the cut:

- cooperativism,
- individualism,
- elitarianism,
- bureaucratism.

The common characteristic of these social orders is the fact that that they emerge and develop from everyday human behavior and style, i.e. from how people solve the problems of their daily subsistence and how they obtain the necessities for life. Because humans' everyday needs and the methods to satisfy them have not particularly changed over the millennia, social order has also remained unchanged through time. Differences emerge due only to the progress of knowledge and technical skills and the human race's ever-improving ability to engage in cooperation to achieve common goals.

Social orders are distinguished from each other by the method their bearers use to obtain the necessities for their daily subsistence and the way they make the decisions that affect their society. Based upon these characteristics, the interest group representing each order can be characterized as follows.

The original representatives of the **cooperativist** order lived off the fruits of their natural-economy labors, engaged in cooperation within the nomad or village community to ensure their subsistence, and participated in democratic decision-making processes that ascertained the common interests of the society and the covering of expenses incurred with enactment of the decisions.

In a broader context, or in a modern society, this social order denotes a society of free people who make the decisions affecting the members of society democratically. In circumstances of a specialization-based market economy, members of this social order assemble into cooperatives, i.e. they implement a form of enterprise in which the owners and the users of the services are the same persons. The natural economy manifests in this case in the process of being forced to participate in the decision-making process of the organizations they own and which services they consume.

Members of the **individualistic** order initiate changes, specialize, and produce products and services by division of labor, exchange them by way of market-economy relationships, and gather into one area, thus laying the foundation for an urban lifestyle. The central focus of the individualistic social order is the freedom of self-realization and the purpose of increasing well-being and wealth.

Members of the **elitarian** order organize military expeditions and other actions or schemes to acquire profits and capital, rule the capital that they possess, and rent it out to subjects who have preserved the right to a independent existence, or they completely enslave the population. Capital ownership and the right to impose taxes brings about a vertical division of labor, a class society, and a military state that defends and fortifies the prevailing injustice. Characteristic of the elitarian governmental culture is the writing of chronicles to document the deeds of the conquerors and secure the privilege of ruling the society for their descendants.

Members of the **bureaucratist** order are government officials whose duty it is to fulfill the role of an impartial third party in interpersonal conflicts, organize economic relations in a market-economy society, and enforce the legal system in a territorial state. Because these officials are responsible for the collection of taxes and the efficiency of their use of state budget funds, they play a decisive role in the organization of the territorial and modern state, and a determinative role in the social state. The rest of the population, more precisely the citizens, submits to their will in exchange for a safe living environment, reasonable opportunities for subsistence, and enforcement of the law.

If we exclude the earliest emergence of civilizations, when the community- and natural-economy-type organization of society was predominant, we see that at all times, in all places, independent of language, culture, and religion, there have existed people who belonged to one of these social orders. However, nations and states are distinguished from each other by the fact that the number of representatives of each of these social orders, the mutual relationships between these groups, and their proportions differ. They might also change in time (but not necessarily). For self-realization, each social order creates the institutions that are characteristic only for this one and exercises only those policies that are inherent to itself. This makes it possible for us, by studying institutions and policies, to indirectly evaluate the mutual relationships and follow the resulting processes of evolution within these societies. There is also the opposite approach: when setting goals and hoping to achieve them, the balance of power and the relationships that exist between the social orders must be taken into account when planning and executing policy.

What follows is an introduction to each social order, where we ascertain which problems in which sphere of life enjoy the most focus in each order. In the next e-book, I shall review the characteristic solutions offered by each social order as well as alternatives to each, according to spheres of life and types of policies.

COOPERATIVISM

THE NATURE OF THE SPIRIT OF COOPERATION

Figure 6. In the two-dimensional approach to social theroy, cooperativism is located on the upper left, i.e. it arises from the voluntary cooperation of free people. By: Paul Tammert

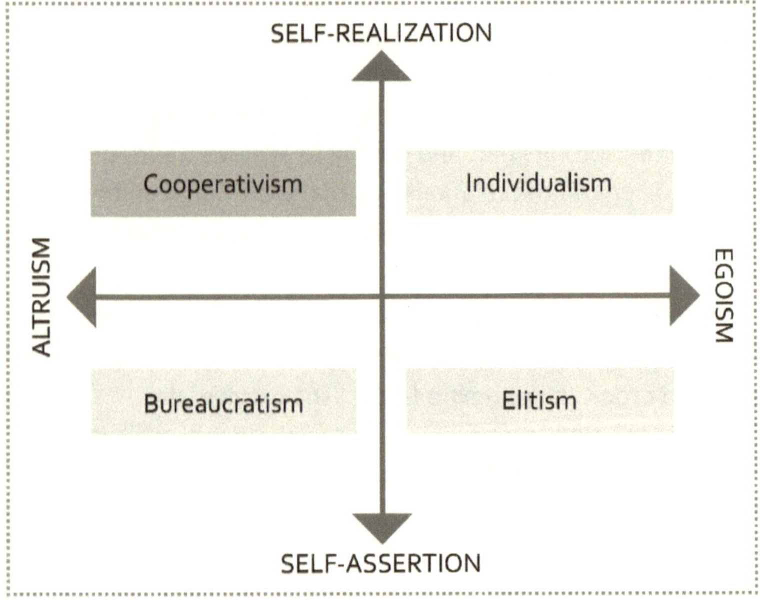

A solitary human is defenseless in the wilds of nature as well as among other members of his species. A human being is born and grows up among other humans. Since primeval times, a human has had to be part of a community that, as a united force, diminished

84

the risks that came with existence. If a person did not belong to a group or don't bear a tribal mark, that individual was helpless and alone. A tribal marking let the potential attacker know that revenge would be forthcoming. The precondition for survival and security was solidarity and mutually assistive cooperation.

Cooperation originates from essentially free people who are forced to engage in cooperation to survive confrontation with the elements and predators. A solitary person is unable to remain on guard for 24 hours a day, 365 days a year, or to protect oneself from external attacks, supply oneself with food and clothing and erect a shelter for protection from climatic impacts. However, with cooperation, this all becomes possible, and the larger the number of cooperating people, the greater are the things they can accomplish. Therefore, we can assert that cooperativism is the most elementary and most widespread form of social existence for humankind throughout history.

People who have lived alone, including in the stories of neglected or lost children (e.g. Rudyard Kipling's Mowgli in *The Jungle Book*) and people who have found themselves in isolation (Daniel Defoe's *Robinson Crusoe*) have demonstrated time and again that a human being must cooperate with others in order to survive, and to feed and defend oneself. As sexual beings, humans cannot reproduce or satisfy their emotional needs without other soulful creatures. Most importantly – intellectual/spiritual self-realization is possible only in a society in which people can achieve a sense of satisfaction while operating within it and receiving its recognition.

In sociology, to be considered a "group" the following criteria must be met:

- there exists a sense of belonging and identification with each other;

- unique social relationships exist between the members of the group;
- the members of the group are mutually dependent on one another;
- there is an understanding within the group that the behavior of every member affects the other members of the group.

A fundamental problem for humans, as material beings, is the contradiction that arises between the body's drive to satisfy physical needs and the soul's drive to satisfy emotional needs as well as the desire for self-realization and, on the other hand, the cognized conviction that these needs can be effectively satisfied only with membership in some human grouping or community.

The concept of "cooperation" denotes the practice in which separate, essentially independent, organisms form groups comprising separate individuals who begin to engage in cooperation:

- to ensure their survival and reap additional benefits from the scale effect when competing with creatures of their own or other species;
- on the principle of mutual benefit, exchanging products of their life's labors with organisms of another species (symbiosis, mutualism).

Because terms pertaining to world view and political ideologies have attached the suffix *-ism*, I shall use the concept of "cooperativism" here as well.

Strengths and Weaknesses of Cooperation

Primitive humans already realized that the group was stronger than its individual members separately. However, cooperation is not natural for the egoistic human, acting for the purpose of keeping one's physical body alive. Only the fear of death forces humans to abandon egoistic self-interest and seek opportunities for working together.

Cooperation inevitably causes conflicts, either because the desires, preferences and needs of people differ, or because they want to keep something that cannot be shared. This gives rise to the question: who is in the right; whose will should prevail? A more detailed overview of the evolution of the concept of administration of justice can be found in the segment entitled "Legal Policy" in the section on bureaucratism, but it must be noted that "justice" is a human idea. And when human ideas come into conflict, there are two possible lines of action:

- to mutually acknowledge each other's rights, but realizing that if these rights cannot be satisfied as they exist, the parties must be prepared to make concessions and engage in negotiation to find a compromise solution that is acceptable to all parties;
- being convinced of the absolute nature of one's right, and considering negotiations to be a sign of weakness, and voluntary abandonment of something to be damaging to one's dignity, the parties begin to fight each other for the right, not stopping until one or both of the parties is killed.

The first solution lays the foundation for a democratic way of decision-making and is an inevitable part of a lifestyle that respects individual freedom and self-organization. The second solution paves the way to an elitarian form of government and guides society down a completely different path of development.

A group that develops from cooperation between people is stronger and more successful than a single individual in every possible sense. The larger the group becomes, the greater potential it acquires, but this potential might remain unused if the group is unable to satisfy its members' needs. Free people are able to engage in effective cooperation only if the group takes its members' interests into account when making decisions. The prerequisite for successful cooperation is achieved when the group

- guarantees equal opportunities for subsistence to its members,
- resolves interpersonal conflicts justly,
- maintains solidarity among members to ensure sustainability of the group as a whole,
- instills in its members a willingness to make altruistic sacrifices if the existence or sustainability of the group should become endangered.

Finding a suitable solution presumes negotiations and a democratic way of decision-making. We often hear the expression "man is a wolf to his fellow man", meaning that everyone proceeds from one's own interests and fails to consider the interests of others. However, imagine two soccer teams, where the members of one team concentrate only on self-realization and every player tries to get the ball into his own possession, in order to kick it into the opposing team's goal net and then enjoy the roaring cheers and overall admiration of the spectators; and the members of the other team, whose members have learned to cooperate and play in a coordinated manner, passing the ball to each other so that it gets to the team member with the best chance of breaking through the opposing team's defensive line and scoring a goal.

Clearly, it is not hard for the reader to discern which of these teams will enjoy an overwhelming win. The team with each member making a solo effort may comprise the best players in the world, but when each one acts only out of self-interest and personal well-being, they may come into excellent position for scoring a goal, but still fail to score the winning point because nobody passes the ball to them at the suitable moment. A team comprising mediocre players but directing its playing strategy at the team member most likely to shoot for the goal, and continuing to pass the ball to him, is much more likely to win. Such cooperation is possible when all the members of the group share the benefits of the victory.

A prerequisite for successful cooperation is the willingness of the individual to make sacrifices and act altruistically. It is equally important for the group to take the interests of its members into consideration and avoid hurting their subsistence or well-being with its actions, otherwise they might just leave. A society whose members value only personal well-being and pleasures, and refuse to make sacrifices, sets out on the path to self-destruction and loses everything. Inability to adapt and unwillingness to respond to changes in the physical, social and economic environment in a timely manner has led to the disappearance of entire nations and states from the arena of history. The strength and sustainability of cooperativism depends on the ability of society's members to understand the situation and make decisions democratically, i.e. to implement collective wisdom.

DEVELOPMENT OF THE SPIRIT OF COOPERATION

The cooperative form of organization has its roots in primitive communities where the form is typical for people who have not yet developed intellectual self-awareness and who seek parental guardianship from the organization. This situation can be compared to the infant in the womb and the period after birth, when the person's own ego and independent self-awareness have not yet developed. In his book *Up from Eden*, Ken Wilber (1949), founder of transpersonal psychology and the integral theory of consciousness, calls it the archetype of primitive awareness or preconsciousness, having the primordial mythical symbol of Ouroboros (depicting a serpent or dragon eating its own tail, thus creating a circle). In human society, this cooperative way of life is represented by the family, tribe, clan, or other forms of cohabitation based on blood ties, as well as many forms of enterprise and social organization in which people confront dangers in the external environment by supporting each other.

The mark of cooperativism is the integral, self-organizing community that relies on collective wisdom and makes decisions democratically. In this context, the concept of "community" denotes a group of people characterized by a common lifestyle with which economic subsistence is guaranteed in a wild or dangerous living environment. This same concept has also evolved within a historical context and acquired different meanings in different environments and in different periods of history. In general, we can recognize the characteristics of a community to be the following:

- It is a network that develops from the mutual influences among the people comprising the group, whereby these relationships permeate the community in all directions and strengthen its members reciprocally (differently from the relationship between two individuals or linear relationships);
- It has a culture based on its own language and customs, founded on a set of common value judgments, meanings and legal norms that are bound by a common history and the identity that is born of it.

American sociologist David E. Pearson (born 1953) mark in the book *International Encyclopedia of Economic Sociology*

(Chapter: Communitarism) that "to earn the appellation of 'community,' it seems to me, groups must be able to exert moral suasion and extract a measure of compliance from their members. That is, communities are necessarily, indeed, by definition, coercive as well as moral, threatening their members with the stick of sanctions if they stray, offering them the carrot of certainty and stability if they don't."

A community-based organization of society, in this context, denotes primarily the primitive, natural-economy village society of foragers, nomads or tillers that must deal with ordeals inflicted by natural forces and cataclysms, as well as competition from other similar communities who might desire the same living space or natural goods.

Formation of a community is characterized by members adopting only those rules and actions that become legal norms once they are firmly entrenched. These norms can be overt or concealed. Overt or official legal norms evolve in the course of the group's common activities, and they are publicly proclaimed or recorded so that all its members can adhere to them. Covert norms are the customs, traditions and beliefs that are passed from one generation to the next during the process of upbringing, and they form an important part of the lifestyle that is characteristic of this group specifically.

Communities are distinguished from each other by the language that they use and the culture that is based on the language. These lay the foundation for mutual understanding and create a feeling of solidarity. Since ancient times, people have ascertained each other's group membership and social status through language, more specifically dialect or manner of speaking. A community's culture is strongly influenced by the successes and failures of its ancestors, as well as the behavioral models, magical rituals, and national traditions that have emerged therefrom.

Community culture is also strongly influenced by the world view adopted and carried forward by the community, and the beliefs that have sprung from this world view.

The advancement of human awareness contributes to the growth of cooperativism's sphere of activity, which becomes territorial. Egoistic people who have achieved self-awareness and reached the developmental stage of independent thinking must also engage in cooperation to diminish subsistence-related risks and preserve a safe living environment; this becomes apparent in the increase of the number of persons engaged in the democratic decision-making process. Cooperative action and the democratic decision process grow gradually; they first take root at the local government level and then the state level, and finally – clearly in the distant future – spread to encompass the entire world. Achievement of the latter is the most difficult, because it is difficult for nations speaking different languages to understand each other, to recognize the cultural behavior models that differ from one's own and enter into trusting relationships with other nations.

THE COMMON WISDOM OF THE COMMUNITY

The foundation of the cooperativist organization of society is the common wisdom of community members. The fact that a community lifestyle engaging in more or less democratic decision-making has existed since the beginning of time is referenced by anthropological studies on aboriginal peoples still living as foragers today. Why has the democratic way of life proved to be so successful and managed to endure all the tests of time?

One of the earliest scientific examples of the people's collective wisdom comes from 1906 England. Sir Francis Galton

(1822–1911), one of the founders of the statistical research method, attended an agricultural fair, where his attention was drawn to a game, organized for the entertainment of the guests, to guess the weight of an ox. Nearly 800 submitted a written guess, with none being able to guess the correct weight of the ox (542.9 kg). However, when he calculated the statistical mean of the submitted guesses, it was 543.4 kg – a stunningly precise result. Galton named this "the voice of the people," which, in today's lingo, would be called "popular opinion".

In his book *The Smart Swarm*, American journalist and National Geographic reporter Peter Miller (born 1934) describes the work of scientists who have studied the behavior of insect swarms and flocks of animals and birds. All the scientists had noticed that due to plentiful mutual influences, there developed a collective approach to problem-solving, conflicting opinions on solutions, democratic decision-making processes, and decentralized organization of leadership.

Jeff Severts (born 1970), vice-president of the American company Best Buy, after listening to a talk by James Surowiecki, author of *The Wisdom of Crowds* about the wisdom of the masses, decided to check its veracity on the employees in his business. At the end of January 2005, he sent an e-mail to hundreds of Best Buy employees asking them to predict how many gift cards the company would sell in February. He received 192 responses. In early March, Severts compared the predictions to the February sales numbers. The accuracy of the collective prediction was 99.5%, which was nearly 5% more accurate than that of the sales projections team. "I was surprised at how eerily accurate the crowd's estimates were", summarized Severts.

Surowiecki explained this phenomenon like this: "If you ask a large enough group of diverse, independent people to make a prediction or estimate a probability, and then average those estimates, the errors each of them makes in coming up with an answer will cancel themselves out. Each person's guess, you might say, has two components: information and error. Subtract the error, and you're left with the information."

Scott E. Page, economist at the University of Michigan, also studied decision-making in communities and found that success was assured by the diversity of knowledge among the members of the community, because this diversity offers a broader base of knowledge about the event being analyzed and possible directions for advancement, as well as information from multiple perspectives. Supplementary knowledge is offered by differing world view, profession and sex. The same principle is used to select United States juries, who are tasked with deciding, based on their own sense of justice, whether defendants are guilty of the crime of which they are accused.

In a word, the guarantor of success for the group-based decision process is diversity, independence, and the combining of various points of view. If, in the course of the decision process, friendly competition of ideas is encouraged and an effective mechanism is applied to narrow the choices, success is guaranteed. Surowiecki summarizes the issue like this: "However, in implementing collective wisdom, people are still inferior to a swarm of bees, because we will continue to think with a brain based on the self-centeredness of the cave dweller."

And like the studies conducted by Argentina's Joaquin Navajas of Torcuato Di Tella University revealed in 2015, the mean of all the estimates submitted by groups divided into teams is even more accurate.

Democracy

The meaning of democracy is derived from the Greek words *"democ"* ("people, crowd") and *"kratos"* ("power, rule"), which, taken together, refer to rule by the people. In his work *Politics*, the ancient Greek philosopher Aristotle (384–322 B.C.) used the compound work *"dēmokratia"* to mean the system of decision-making and governance that included the citizens of the city of Athens. It should be emphasized that the word *"demos"* denoted Athenian adult male real estate owners who were heads of families, paid taxes to the city, and personally (with their own equipment) participated in defending the city and engaging in its more distant military actions. This means that only 10% of the population of Athens participated in political decision-making, although everyone born in Athens enjoyed a citizens' rights.

Disputes over the meaning of rule by the people, i.e. who has the right and authority to make decisions about how the members of society should behave and organize their lives, have been taking place since the beginning of time. And they will obviously continue into the future, for as long as such societies exist. A study of history reveals that only those people who demonstrated willingness to defend their own property and the common property of the community, even with their lives, who were capable to understanding what was going on around them, were able to grasp the issues affecting the community, and could successfully organize its economic relations, participated in democratic decision-making processes. Therefore, it is hardly surprising that the democracy of the ancient and Middle Ages actually meant the power of tribal, military and religious leaders, and in city-states, of a narrow circle of businessmen – the power of those who were able to cover the costs of activities serving the public interest.

The earliest written references to a democratic form of government originate from the Sumerian city-states (third century B.C.). Cuneiform tablets tell us of a two-chamber parliament and the discussions that were held there (Samuel Noah Kramer. Histrory Begins at Sumer). A circular stepped auditorium that may have been the location of such discussions has been excavated at the city of Mari on the middle course of the Euphrates River.

After the Aryan tribes invaded (about 1800 B.C.) and secured their supremacy, 16 territorial units (Mahajanapadas) were formed on the territory of Northern India (about 700 B.C.), the largest being Magadha, Kosala and Vaishal (today's Bihar). By nature, these were oligarchic representative democracies, because members of the council were elected from the priest (Brahmin) class. The administrative organization of today's Indian villages is based on this panchayat system.

In Sparta, a voting-based elections system came into use about 700 B.C.; males aged 30 or more with warrior status could participate. In the city-state of Athens, the noble and statesman Cleisthenes enacted a direct-democracy system of government when he reformed the organization of the government. Rome was also governed by a representative-democracy system: the practice of holding plebiscites (direct democracy) was established as early as the royal period. After proclamation of the Republic in 509 B.C., power was transferred to the Senate, comprising tribal elders who made decisions on the principle of majority democracy. Medieval Italian city-states, such as Venice, Genoa, Florence, Pisa, Lucca, Amalfi, Siena and San Marino were governed by democratic representative bodies. A territorial self-government based on direct democracy was born in the Tirolean region of Switzerland (Swiss Confederacy) in 1291.

Gatherings of tribal elders and warlords, and decision-making by vote (representative and majority democracy), were used among ancient and early Middle Ages Germanic tribes (Thing, first mentioned in the year 193), in Norway (Frostating), England (Witenagemot, 849), Iceland (Althing, 930–1799), the regions of the Frisian tribes (tenth to fifteenth centuries), Faroe Islands (Løgtingið, 1274–1816), and others.

In the Slavic tribal regions, new princes were elected democratically in Carantania (in today's Slovenia, seventh to fifteenth centuries), state affairs were decided at public meetings in Pskov (Veche, 862–1510), Novgorod (1016–1478) and Kiev (1068–1240), as well as Polish–Lithuanian Rzeczpospolita (sejm, 1180, 1569–1795).

In the Arab world, the Rashidun ("rightly guided", 632–661) caliphate made its mark on history with its democratic organization of government. It included all of the Persian, Middle Eastern, and Northern African areas all the way to Tunisia. A group of elders that made their decisions democratically helped to rule the regions of the Nakh tribes (in the Northern Caucasus, the territory of today's Chechnya and Ingushia), the Nri tribe (in Nigeria 948–1911), the territory of the Sikhs (starting in the tenth century), the commercial city of Sakai (Japan 1450–1600), and other regions.

The process by which the council comprising the ruling elite (i.e. tribal elders, warlords and high clerics) became a legislative institution got its start in England. The landowning liege lords protested the tax burden imposed by their autocrat and, in 1215, forced the propertyless King John I, also known as John Lackland (1166–1216) to sign the Magna Carta, in which the king recognized the right of the liege lords to decide whether the royally imposed tax obligation should become a legal obligation or not. The actual English Parliament was born in 1265, when King Edward I (1254–1299) faced a rebellion of landowners against the taxes levied on them; they were led by Baron Simon de Montfort (1208–1265), and they forced the reluctant ruler to recognize the landowners' representative body as a legislative institution.

The Magna Carta established a free trade zone encompassing the entire island by prohibiting the collections of customs duties at the borders of royal and liege lord properties. This paved the way for the advancement of manufacturing and trade, which in turn led to growing wealth for the urban citizenry. And since – naturally – tax revenues can be collected from places where profit is being earned and wealth is being accumulated, the king felt a growing desire to tax the newly wealthy enterpreneurs. However, because the Magna Carta had enacted the principle of "no taxation without representation", the English parliament was enlarged in 1341 with the establishment of the Lower House, which began representing the new taxpayers: the urban citizenry. In those Western European commercial towns that had acquired the status of free cities, city councils were established to represent the larger guilds of craftsmen and merchants, in addition to the local tribal chief, military leaders and clergy.

The next evolutionary leap for democracy – the expansion of political rights – occurred after the Industrial Revolution, when salaried factory work became predominant and the tax revenues collected from this employment income rose to be the most significant source of income for the new territorial states. First, suffrage was extended to men engaged in salaried work, and later – to a great degree because of the two world wars that ravaged Europe, during which women entered the circle of salaried workers – to women as well.

The further expansion of democracy inside the social state has begun to endanger its original concept because, with the general expansion of suffrage, the proportion of those people with no tax obligations but still receiving appropriations from the state budget in the form of various benefits, has increased among the voting population. The opportunity to receive benefits without obligations has allowed the emergence and expansion of populist politics, because poorly-educated people have never understood the cause-and-effect relationship and have never been interested in participating in complex, topic-specific discussions. A mass of simple-minded, avaricious people is easy to excite emotionally, to the point where it can destroy everything in its path, like an avalanche, including democracy itself.

The first Republican president of the United States, Abraham Lincoln (1809–1865), explained the meaning of democracy like this: "Democracy is government of the people, by the people, for the people." Irish playwright George Bernard Shaw (1856–1950) noted: "Democracy is a device that insures we shall be governed no better than we deserve." Pakistani politician and the first female prime minister of an Islamic state Benazir Bhutto (1953–2007) stated: "Democracy is the best revenge." British prime minister Winston Churchill (1874–1965) voiced the oft-quoted definition: "Democracy is the worst form of government, except for all the others." This last claim can be explained by saying that democracy allows the nation to peaceably correct its mistake, if it has elected the wrong people. However, if the masses re-elect leaders who make their lives hell, then that is exactly what they deserve! In every other system of government, the position of ruler is for a lifetime, which can ruin the lives of people for entire generations.

Actually, humankind has, to this day, been unable to agree on the clear and exact definition of democracy, legal equality, political freedom and legal order. In his book *In Search of Democracy*, American political scientist Larry Jay Diamond (1951) has described four important factors that are characteristic of democracy.

- Every adult citizen has the right to participate in free and fair elections where executors of governmental authority are elected for a predetermined period.

- Citizens participate actively in political life and the organization of civil society.
- Citizens' human rights and personal property are protected.
- The state is run by constitutional rule of law, which guarantees equal treatment of all citizens.

The concept of freedom is based on the presumption that every person has the sovereign right to decide for themselves how they will live and how they will organize their lives. However, if people want to receive protection or other benefits from the social organization or the state, they must also participate in covering the expenses of those benefits. Participation in covering public expenses gives the person the right to a voice regarding the use of collected tax revenues. And this right is realized in some form of democracy. The essential problem of democracy is how to ascertain the will of the people when the nation comprises many individuals, each with their own interests and their own understanding of what is right.

THE FIELD OF ACTIVITY OF COOPERATIVISM

The specific form of cooperativism as a social order arises as a combination of two antithetical forces driven by

- **freedom of the individual** to satisfy the objective needs dictated by one's physical body and the subjective needs dictated by one's soul and intellect;
- **the equal right of all people** to use the resources owned by the community or the state (land, natural resources, etc.) and to participate in the decision-making process that defines the community's common interests and determines how to satisfy them.

Here we must admit that the freedom of self-realization is most important from the individual's standpoint, and the necessity of ensuring subsistence opportunities for everyone is most important from the community sustainability standpoint. In this case, freedom and equality stand opposite. The greater the freedom of individual self-realization, the more difficult it is to ensure the equality of all people, and vice versa: material equality can be increased only by limiting individual freedoms in some way! Equality increases when people become organized and begin to act as a group. As the power of the group over its members grows, each individual's opportunity to pursue what they want shrinks. This situation is well characterized by the old saying: "The road to hell is paved with good intentions."

Thus, cooperativism focuses on finding an optimal solution, i.e. a balance between the common interests of the community and the private interests of the individual. It is important to emphasize that this is a never-ending process, because with the cyclical and noncyclical changes in the natural environment, as well as the continuous developments within society, this balance always tends to go "off kilter". Time and again, the community must re-ascertain its common interests and formalize them in the legislative institution as the public will.

The balance between individual and group interests should be sought in a way that makes essentially free and independent individuals want to participate in the group and remain its members. This means that the group's common interest and sustainability must not be placed above the private interests of its members. Exceeding the "pain threshold" of group members should be avoided because, if it is not, they will leave the group, which will weaken the group's ability to support and sustain itself. In today's world, departure from a group is most often manifested by the desire of young people at their best working age to leave their country. They are driven by the desire to find a better country and society for their self-realization.

Let us take a closer look at the models of democracy that could be implemented to ensure equality, and how great a proportion of people will have their need for self-realization taken into consideration in these models.

Forms of Democracy on the Axis of Equality

Figure 7. Cooperativism is based on a democratic way of decision-making. As we move from right to left on the axis of equality, i.e. toward the expansion of representation and increase of voter participation, the forms of democracy are: representative democracy > delegative democracy > direct democracy. By: P. Tammert.

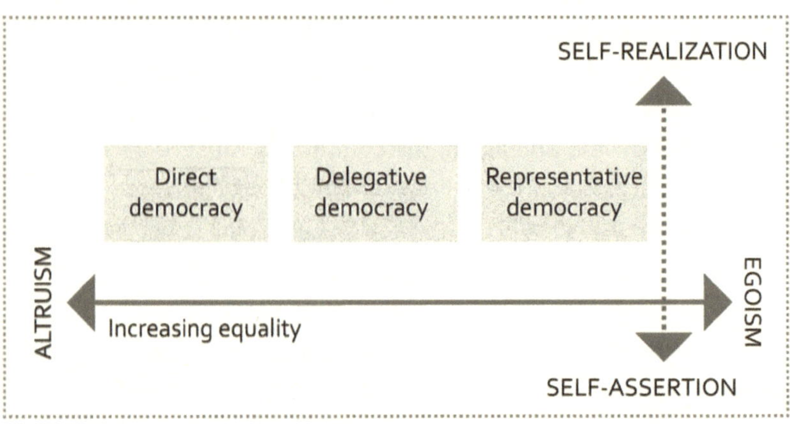

The segments of the equality axis in the cooperativism sector are distinguished from each other by the form of democratic discussion, i.e. the way that the members of society participate in the decision-making process, and their rights in this process.

In the case of **direct democracy**, all persons with the right to vote may participate in discussion and voting; however, their number may be limited by some attribute. For example, the right to participate in these processes might be enjoyed by only the following: tribal and military leaders, land- or property owners, taxpayers, only men, or all persons who have reached a certain age.

In **representative democracy**, voters have only the right to elect their representative. Subsequently, their opportunities to influence the decisions, made by representatives, are very small or actually non-existent.

In **delegative democracy**, interest groups send their representatives to a legislative institution while maintaining control over their delegates' activities with the right to recall them at any time. This, in turn, provides everyone with the opportunity, but not the obligation, to participate actively in the legislative process, because the elected representative must, in fear of losing the public's trust, continue to discuss and achieve consensus on the decisions that are put to vote. This also gives the electorate the liberty of choosing whether or not they want to have a voice in the decision process for any specific decision. Interest groups are formed not only on the basis of world-view ideology, but also on the basis of actual economic interests (as for groups of teachers, farmers, medical workers, government officials, enterpreneurs, etc.).

Degrees of Democracy on the Axis of Freedom

The segments of the freedom axis are defined by what percentage of those people who have participated in the discussion and voting process have had their needs satisfied by a democratically made decision. If the decision satisfies

- 51–65%, it is called **majority democracy**.

- 66–89%, it could be called **accommodational or compromise democracy**. This topic has been dealt with in depth by Lars-Göran Stenelo and Magnus Jemeck in their book *The Bargaining Democracy*.
- 90–100% of the voters, it is consensus democracy.

Figure 8. Cooperativism arises from the will of the citizens. If we move from the bottom up on the freedom axis, i.e. toward the expansion of the majority, the forms of democracy are: majority democracy > compromise democracy > consensus democracy. By: P. Tammert.

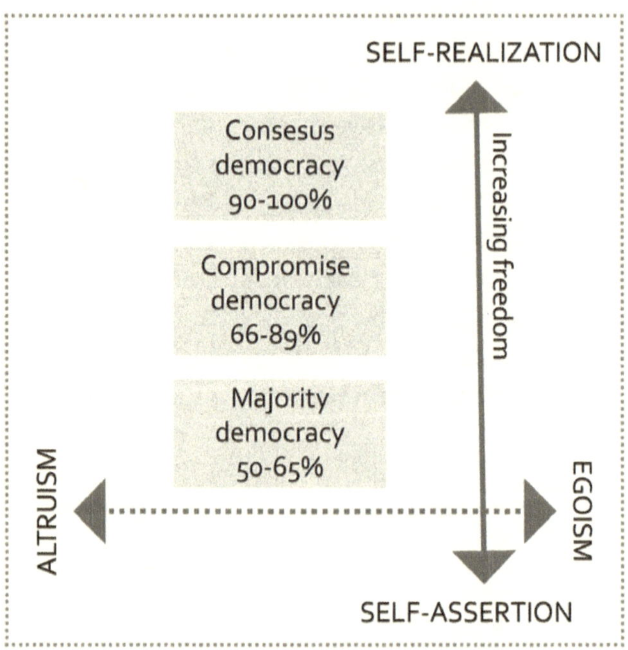

INDIVIDUALISM

Figure 9. Individualism is located at the upper right of the two-dimensional approach (axes of equality and freedom) to social theory. It is based on the self-realization of free people in a market-economy environment in which the magnitude of egoism determines the economic model. By: P. Tammert.

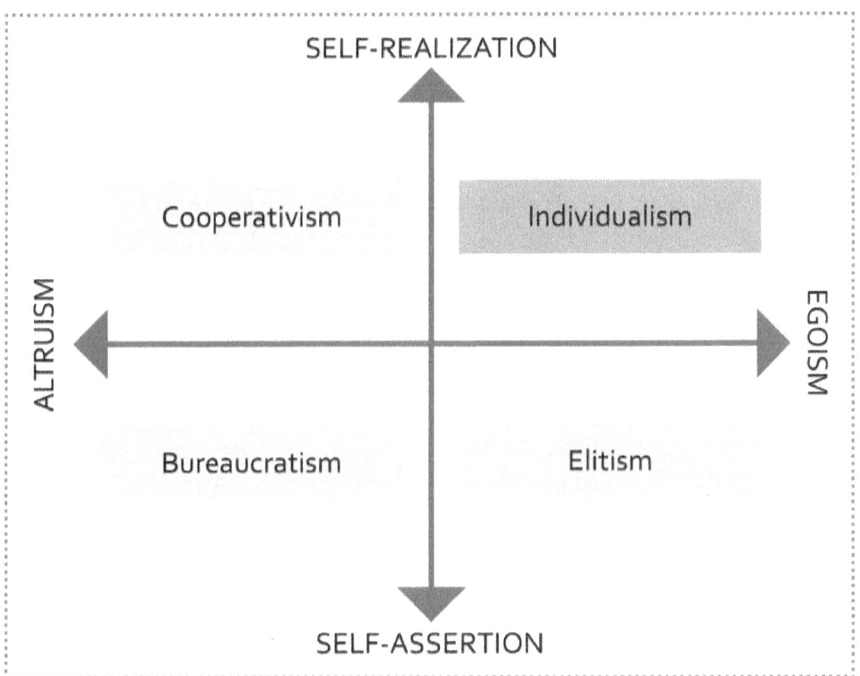

SELF-AWARENESS

The concept of "individualism", which denotes a behavior model based on individual self-realization, is derived from the Latin word *"individuum"* ("indivisible entity, individual human") with the suffix -ism to form a derivative denoting an ideology.

Self-awareness refers to the fact that humans, in their intellectual evolution, have risen above the level of the animal kingdom's sensory consciousness and purely instinctual behavior, and have become aware of themselves as independent and self-sufficient individuals. The first sign of self-awareness is the recognition of one's reflection and the association of oneself with the body that is visible in the mirror. In children, the birth of self-awareness becomes evident when the child's manner of speaking changes: they stop talking about themselves in the third person and gradually, but ever more forcefully, begins to express the will of their "self".

Consciousness of the self originated in Western Europe with René Descartes' (1596–1650) expression of "I think, therefore I am", and was formulated in the discussions of Jean-Jacques Rousseau (1712–1778), in which he compared the "self-loving" (*amour de soi*) person who is self-interested and does not see themselves as others do, and the "self-loving" (*amour-propre*) person whose esteem depends upon the opinion of others.

In the analytical philosophy of mind, conditions of subjective experience and cognition are referred to as the phenomenological attributes named qualia. The word "quale" is derived from the Latin word *"quale"* ('of what sort, of what kind'). The concept of qualia was first brought into use by the American philosopher Clarence Irving Lewis (1883–1964) in 1929. Qualia arise from perceived sensations, abstract feelings, perception of the environment, and sometimes from the thoughts of other persons. Philosophers as well as scientists study the connections between qualia and perception of the external environment, as well as the problems of mind and consciousness, and body and spirit. The greatest conundrum in relation to qualia is that they do not exist in the physical or material sense. They can be ascertained and studied only by way of subjective, sensual reactions, in the context of "how does it feel to …?".

Based upon the theories of psychoanalyst Sigmund Freud (1856–1939), Ken Wilber distinguishes three components in the development of human self-awareness:

- Id – originating from feelings and based upon instinct; the original, unorganized human character (English "it", German "*es*", Estonian "*see*"), that refers to itself, at best, in the third person.

- Ego – self-awareness that perceives the surrounding reality and is self-aware, and which has separated from preconsciousness, become aware of one's own existence and mortality, and attempts to forestall or even deny death by engaging in self-realization (English "I", German "*Ich*", Estonian "*mina*").

- Super-ego – the combination of one's ego and the "conscience" that reflects culture acquired from the environment (through personal experience, education, mass and social media, and other sources) (German "*über-Ich*" Estonian "*ülimina*").

The human ego, for which I will here use the word "self", binds the physical circumstances that one has experienced and survived and emotional experiences into one entity, with which it identifies. The nature of self-awareness is determined by the events it has interpreted as well as that which remains hidden in the subconscious. Life wisdom crystallizes from interpreted experiences, and this helps the person make reasoned decisions and avoid repeating previous mistakes in the future. The uninterpreted experiences remaining in the subconscious give rise to negative emotions and illnesses and make the person's behavior unpredictable. A person's self-image shapes one's treatment of incoming information and becomes the nucleus for the development of one's personality.

THE EFFECT OF SPECIALIZATION

The foundation of the individualistic social order is the person who is achieving self-realization through specialization and who is striving to improve one's material well-being by oneself. Specialization means distinction from the common activities of society by focusing on one job for self-serving reasons. Whether individualistic specialization is good or bad has been a topic of contention throughout history, and this argument will probably continue into the future, because with its multifaceted nature, it has paved the way for so many developments that it reminds us of "Pandora's box". In the chapter "Homo Domesticus" of the book *The Greeks*, James Redfield (born 1935) presents a summary of the Hesiod story, which illustrates the effect of specialization on humankind very well:

> *At first, life was simple: people could live an entire year from one day's work, and the gods and humans celebrated together. One day, one of the guests, Prometheus, divided the meat into inequitable portions. He took the meat and hide and placed them into an ox's stomach, while taking a large pile of bones and wrapping them in fat. When Zeus claimed that such a division seemed unfair, Prometheus allowed him to choose between the portions. Although Zeus realized that*

It is the same case with individualization, i.e. distancing oneself from Nature and the community, and adopting specialization. By adopting a new way of life and focusing on one job, human productivity increases and the resources available to society become more plentiful; this improves human life to an unprecedented degree. However, the increase of wealth is accompanied by the growth of greed and other afflictions arising from abundance. There develops the need for a third party – an impartial resolver of conflicts. This need gave rise to administrators of justice, from whom the institution of courts evolved. Because cities have a perpetual need for administration of justice due to their large population, and the demand for this service grows along with the growth of the city, it gives rise to yet another form of specialization – officials representing the common interests of the city dwellers. These officials differ from the rest of the citizenry because they must set aside personal interests, and they are remunerated for their work with fees paid by the parties who request and use their services. The initiators of the dispute must pay the judge a predetermined amount or a certain percentage of the value of the object of the dispute.

It must also be noted than an individualistic lifestyle is possible only in a secure living environment that maintains legal order and eliminates crime.

INNOVATION AND TECHNICAL PROGRESS

The forces that drive society's economic development are the human's egoistic desires: to eat more and better food, wear better clothes, live more comfortably, continue to encounter and enjoy new experiences, and possess greater reserves to minimize future risks. All progress arises from the desire to do something differently, better, more effectively with less cost of materials, energy and labor. When somebody does something in a new way and better than others, resulting in greater income, it means that somebody somewhere is losing something. This brings about disagreements and conflicts. The losers see diminished opportunities to sell their labor or fruits thereof, i.e. they see dwindling opportunity to obtain profits from their work and use it to cover subsistence costs. The knowledge, skills and equipment of less effective persons, communities, businesses and states lose their value and become useless, forcing them to come up with something new. The successful ones pave the way to a new upward spiral of progress, creating new losers, and those who fail must face poverty when they are left without the resources they need for subsistence. In this way, a market economy paves the way for innovation, on one hand, and for a competitive environment on the other, in which consumers make their choice and determine the winner by their purchases. Supporters of the theory of natural selection feel that this is the way it should be, because losers must leave the arena – die out or, in the economic sense, become bankrupt.

Scottish economist and moral philosopher Adam Smith (1723–1790) described in his fundamental work of 1759 entitled *An Inquiry Into the Nature and Causes of the Wealth of Nations* the concept of the "invisible hand of the market", which guides not only the market, but also the evolution of society. While idealizing market economy, he opposed the privilege of the ruling elite to own land and other means of production that they leased to consumers for predatory prices; he also opposed the limiting of enterpreneurial activity with the distribution of licenses, permits, rights and prohibitions by officials exercising state power, all to protect the interests of the ruling elite. He called this kind of order mercantilism.

To illustrate the advantages of market-economy progress, Adam Smith provides in his book the example of manufacturing pins. Typically, one artisan was able to make one pin in a day, but after the job was divided into 12 different operations (performed by 12 workers) and the process was mechanized, they could produce 48,000 pins in a day. The ever-narrowing specialization has brought productivity to an unprecedented extent! Henry Ford experienced the same when he started to produce cars on the assembly line. Thanks to this new and efficient organization of work, it took Ford 5.75 hours to assemble one car in 1925, while his competitors Morris spent 29 hours, Audi 350, Benz 450, and Daimler 1,750 hours to assemble one car – the latter spending 304 times as much time as Ford to build one automobile.

In a natural-economy society, everyone produces what they can and a quantity as they need. Specialization lay the foundation for a completely novel situation in which there were plenty of goods for all, along with rapidly decreasing cost of production. Despite the fact that the sale price of goods decreased, the profits of the producers increased, because the quantity of goods being sold increased faster. The ones who succeeded in best taking advantage of the scale effect, i.e. by increasing production and sales turnover, seized the market and took away the others' subsistence opportunities. This angered the small-business artisans, culminating in the destruction of machines and factories. In England, the machine-wreckers in 1811–1816 received the name of Luddites, after Ned Ludd, the initiator and leader of the movement.

Individualistic innovation also had a broader social effect, because machines found their way outside the walls of factory buildings and began operating outside, i.e. lifting things, transporting goods, plowing the fields, and doing other difficult work. These machines took the underpinnings of the work and existence away from the natural-economy village community, because now it was cheaper to buy food from the store than to grow it oneself. Thanks to the tractor, the combine, and other such machines, one farmer could cultivate more land by himself than many villages previously working together. Left without a source of subsistence, the uncompetitive village communities collapsed, and people left the countryside.

Specialization and mass production generate a surplus that improves the subsistence and well-being of all people participating in the economic process as well as those closest to them, but also robs those people who want to continue the old ways of their subsistence opportunities. Specialization affects development within the state, as well as on an international scale. Every nation, society or state engaged in international trade must find the spheres in which their existing natural environment and natural resources, geographic location and human capital offer the greatest competitive advantage, and to put them to use. This, precisely, is their freedom, while economic reality spurs on even those who do not wish to take advantage of this freedom. Thus, the competitive environment brought to life by individualistic market economy is very similar to the struggle for existence in nature, where living creatures must adapt to a constantly changing environment or become extinct.

British economist David Ricardo (1772–1823) was self-taught, but his ability to understand economic processes exceeded even that of the professors of his time. The mathematical investigative methods and analytical models he used, as well as his book *On the Principles of Political Economy and Taxation,* lay the foundation for modern economics. His "law of comparative advantage" framed the fundamentals of free market economy. He showed that specialization always improves the performance of enterprise, because the best result is achieved by abandoning less profitable or unprofitable (and therefore uncompetitive) activities. Ricardo's statement in this regard became well-known:

> *If French farmers are willing to feed us for less than it would cost to feed ourselves, let us eat French food and spend our time doing something else. If Santa Claus begins airlifting cakes, cookies, and clothing by reindeer, should we shoot Rudolph out of the sky because we bake and sew ourselves?*

Thus, a low market price can conflict with the manufacturer's high production cost. Those businesses that are unable to sell their products in circumstances of free competition must now close shop without any external coercion. In a free-market environment, the sustainability and competitiveness of of society as a whole depend on its willingness to accept new ideas in a changing environment and to experiment with the solutions they offer. And if it becomes clear that some old customary practice has become obsolete and is interfering with a rational mode of living, it should be discarded and forgotten. Those solutions and technologies that perhaps improve the well-being of some people but inflict such environmental damage that it endangers the very existence of humankind, should also be abandoned.

In his research, Adam Smith reached the conclusion that the price offered for goods on sale on the free market is always fair, because the consumers themselves decide whether the enjoyment obtained from the purchase (environment) and the benefit obtained from consuming the product is in suitable proportion with whatever is given in exchange. After all, it is the consumers who determine in what environment and at what price they will make the purchase, i.e. cheaply off the internet or at the open-air market, or expensively from a super-luxurious department store. The free market guarantees diversity of goods and services, taking into account absolutely all factors affecting the economic environment.

The Market Economy, The City and Legal Order

The market lives according to a simple principle: if someone wants to get something that someone else has worked and labored to produce, then that person must give something that has also been acquired with work and labor in return. If there were a large pile of gold pieces lying on the ground, they would be as valuable as the leaves that fall from the trees. But if this gold is brought out of the earth with work and labor, or if it has been used to make beautiful jewelry, which many people desire, then gold becomes a commodity and acquires value. The value of goods is determined by the consumers themselves, and it is expressed as the relationship between supply and demand.

Individualistic persons must subsist on the sale of the fruits of their labor. Thus, artisans assemble into one place for the more effective sale of their products, and their workshops and stores give rise to commercial streets. Marketplaces have typically emerged somewhere in the area where the local agricultural population gathers on prearranged days to display their wares and conduct transactions of exchange. People establish residential quarters around these commercial streets and marketplaces, and this paves the way for the urban lifestyle. The city, the market, and exchange-based economy are phenomena of the individualist lifestyle.

The first commercial town – Jericho – was established about 9400 B.C. in the Middle East next to a large trade route and still exists today. The second oldest city, Mehrgarh, was founded on the territory of today's Pakistan in about 7000 B.C. This city also rose beside a trade route that joined the food-rich areas of India with the natural resources-rich areas of Afghanistan. From this city, established on the banks of a tributary of the Indus River, arose the Indus Valley Civilization that included the entire river basin; however, it collapsed in about 1700 B.C. The people of Mehrgarh became renowned for their skills in drilling of precious stones and hard materials (including teeth). Jewelry made in this city has been found across a vast area, from China to Egypt. The Indus Valley Civilization included more than 50 cities, the largest of which had populations of up to 40,000. These cities boasted straight streets and stone houses, and had water and sewage systems, public pools and warehousing and harbor facilities.

The greatest ancient cities were established in the region of today's Iraq, and were built up by the Sumerian culture that dominated in the region from 5400 to 2000 B.C. The first city to be established there was <u>Eridu,</u> with a temple at its center. This temple was remarkable because all the subsequently built houses of worship in the Middle East and Europe have been built according to the same basic design. The second-oldest and largest city – <u>Uruk</u> – covered an area of 6 square kilometers and, during its heyday (about 2900 B.C.), it boasted a population of 80,000, or about 0.5% of the Earth's population. In comparison: Shanghai, the largest city in the world today, has a population of 24 million, or 0.32% of the Earth's population, and the population of the entire planet Earth is 7.4 billion (as of August 2016).

Something remarkable for the individualistic social order is a legend preserved in cuneiform on clay tablets telling of the journey of <u>Inanna</u>, the ruler of Uruk as well as the goddess of love, fertility and war, to visit <u>Enki</u>, the god of wisdom, in Eridu. Using her feminine wiles and intoxicating drinks, Inanna enticed Enki to give her more than 100 "<u>me</u>'s", after which she escaped back to her home city. We learn from this legend that it was the use of these "me's" that lay the foundation for the unprecedented growth and influence of Uruk. In his 1956 book entitled *History Begins at Sumer. Thirty-nine Firsts in Recorded History*, <u>Samuel Noah Kramer</u> lists the achievements of civilization implemented by the Sumerian people and which remain the foundation of our culture even today. On the basis of the materials translated from the cuneiform tablets, Kramer described the institution of school and the problems that were present there (relationships between parents and children, bribes given to teachers), the study of nature and the teaching of farming, healing of the sick, activities of a bicameral parliament, the legislative process and the compilation of a written code, the seeking of justice and court actions, conflicts between (city-)states that expanded from a "war of nerves" into military action, protests against high tax obligations, the first tax reform, etc.

Kramer's descriptions are supplemented by <u>Zecharia Sitchin</u> (1920–2010), who introduces in his 1980 book entitled *Genesis Revisited* the Sumerian conception of the world and their knowledge of astronomy. According to these sources, the Sumerians knew all the planets of the solar system, including Uranus and Pluto; they knew of their moons and their appearance (Uranus is blue and Pluto's axis is tilted). We, the people of today, did not learn these facts until the American spaceships Pioneer I and II transmitted photographs of these planets in 1998. The Sumerians also described the creation of Earth as a planet, and a large flood (today's science is still out on these processes), etc. We should also add technological inventions to this list, for instance the potter's wheel and the wagon wheel, fired-clay vessels and glazed earthenware, cultivation with a plow (which simultaneously operated as a seeding machine), the weaving of cloth, using tin oxide to fashion objects from copper ore (bronze), brewing of beer and date wine, etc.

The individualistic nature of Sumerian culture is indicated on millions of cuneiform-covered tablets that include formal contracts of employment, trade, land purchase and sale, as well as others. Such contracts are entered into only by independent subjects or free people, not slaves! And they make up most of the materials found. It is also notable that these contracts originating from the third millennium B.C. include calculations of the area of triangular plots of land. If we compare these inventions, made over a few thousand years, with the progress that took place during the previous hundred thousand years, during which skills with the hand-axe evolved into knowledge of how to make sharp stone shards, we can only be amazed at this burst of innovation that is comparable only to that which took place in the twentieth century.

From the Sumerian cities arose city-states that, after their cultural decline and seizure of their territories by Semitic and Indo-

European nomadic tribes, began to compete among themselves and wage wars of supremacy throughout the entire Middle East. In Mesopotamia, the city of Babylon most decidedly practiced the individualist lifestyle; its population numbered more than 200,000 during its glory days. The Babylonian ruler Hammurabi (1792–1750 B.C.) secured his place in history with a code of law that became a training tool for the judges of the region for more than a thousand years and is still preserved today. It was in Babylon that the Jews who were deported there acquired the principles of an individualistic lifestyle, which they have passed on through their educational system into current times.

After the fall of the city of Babylon, the city-states of Phoenicia and Ancient Greece carried on the individualist lifestyle, with Athens at the forefront, followed by Rome in Italy. After the fall of the Roman Empire, the baton of individualism was passed to the Italian commercial towns of the early Middle Ages. The most noteworthy among them was the Republic of Venice, which dominated the Mediterranean region for more than a millennium. The role of standard-bearer of the individualistic lifestyle was taken from Italy first by Holland, which established its own republic, and then Great Britain, which grew from England and lay the foundation for the Anglo-American culture "on which the sun never sets".

Cities amplify the good and bad qualities of their residents and all of society. The wealth arising from specialized skills and trade served to enhance specialization. Centers for the collection and imparting of knowledge were established in the cities, in turn laying the foundation for the development of architecture and the fine arts, the accomplishments of which we still admire today. However, the ever-greater advancement of well-being, improvement of living standards, and greater opportunities for entertainment brought about a decreasing birth rate, because city dwellers had so much else to do than satisfy their primitive needs.

Family size has always been contingent on standard of living. The higher the standard of living, the smaller the families. Quantity is replaced by quality, the birth rate drops, and the urban population begins to shrink. Therefore cities, if they want to last, must constantly enlarge their population with rural folk. This process has been studied and described in depth by the German historian and philosopher Oswald Spengler (1880–1936) in his book *The Decline of the West* (*Der Untergang des Abendlandes*).

Because the urban environment encouraged progress, differences in the intellectual development level of people became ever more apparent. Some had a better understanding of things; they recognized problems, were capable of solving them, and continued to offer the market new products and services that improved human subsistence and well-being. Because their products were purchased in great quantity, they earned a larger income and became wealthy. Others who were unable to produce anything or to sell what they produced, and did not care to put any physical or intellectual effort into self-improvement, lagged behind the successful ones in this process of advancement, i.e. they earned less income or none at all. This stirred up envy, along with a desire to share some of the well-being established by others, paving the way for crime and the conflicts it causes. Thus, the individualization and specialization that allows humans to depart from a natural-economy society is accompanied by limitless improvement of well-being, but it also creates circumstances for the emergence of all kinds of evil (Pandora's box), which starts to thrive when it escapes society's reins. To limit conflicts caused by greed for profit and to create a sustainable market economy, an integral legal order had to be established, which in turn lay the foundation for the emergence of the state as an institution.

MONEY AND BANKING

Both Smith and Ricardo have emphasized that the development of market economy depends directly on its ability to organize the exchange of goods and services. In a goods-for-goods (barter) economy, achieving an exchange transaction that satisfies both parties are very complicated, because the price relationship between vastly different products is hard to determine, and their exchange at an appropriate moment is all but impossible. Try, for instance, to buy a loaf of bread for your family, when you have a cow to offer in exchange.

An effective exchange economy is possible only when a universal currency, which is also the measure of value, is brought into use. This currency might be anything – it is only important that the people participating in market transactions are able to agree on it and to define the principles for the measure of value. Throughout history, almost everything having any value has been used as currency, as well as things that have no value in themselves: animals and their hides, easily preservable foodstuffs (in Old Egypt, for instance, grain fulfilled the function of money, and granaries served as banks), salt, shells of shellfish, precious stones, etc.

When **metals** came into use, they lay the foundation for a completely new level of development of currencies, because bars of any appropriate size, shape and content could be fashioned of metal. In Sumeria, the droplets of silver that were produced upon pouring molten silver into water were used as currency units. Metal coins of standard form and shape came into use in the Kingdom of Lydia in Asia Minor about 650 B.C. At that time, coined money began serving as the main currency. However, metal coins are heavy and, with robbery being a profitable activity, moving about with coins was dangerous. Therefore, many preferred to deposit their coins in a safe place and use the notes given to them by the

120

money's keeper instead. Such banknotes came into use as currency in Sweden in 1661. Because copper, a relatively inexpensive metal, was plentiful there, the more valuable "coins" could weigh 15 kilograms or more, making them awkward to use in daily trading. The problem was solved rationally: Stockholms Banco, founded by private citizens, accepted the copper bars for deposit and issued (bank)notes in exchange, which were then used as currency.

Over time, it became evident that only one in ten banknote bearers would come in to claim his metal coins. This lay the foundation for banking and allowed the start of an excellent but risky business. Banks emitted notes worth several times the value of the capital they owned, while demanding "fair" payment in return. It was important only that the bank remain liquid, i.e. that it would have, at any given time, enough coins to satisfy any claims. At first, notes worth nine times the value of capital were emitted, but appetite and willingness to take risks increased over time. During the financial crisis of 2008, it was learned that Dexia, a Belgian bank, had bought up the bonds of local governments of various states (i.e. had issued loans), leveraged by a factor of 60–1, rendering the bank unable to pay the claims of their depositors during the crisis situation.

From **bank bonds** developed paper money, which in essence is a guaranteed bond issued by the state's ruler. To guarantee continued trust, a "central bank" had to be established, with the sole right to emit bonds with the government's signature, and able to exchange the bonds for precious metal coins at any given moment. The first such central bank (Bank of England) was established in London in 1694 by royal decree. Private citizens deposited 750,000 pounds sterling, and the bank had the right to emit 10 pounds sterling for every deposited pound sterling. Also, the king obligated the bank to issue him a personal loan of 250,000 pounds sterling to cover state expenses; this was repaid with tax revenues. By 1945, the government's bank debt had grown to 22.5 billion pounds.

The government's demands for issuance of state bonds brought about the uncontrolled emission of money in Germany during World War I, which weakened trust in money, because the quantity of goods on the market stayed the same. For example, in January of 1918, one gold mark (0.35842 g of gold) in Germany could be purchased for one mark, but six years later in 1923, the cost of one gold mark had ballooned to 1,000,000,000,000 German marks (hyperinflation). The value of the German mark fell by a factor of 100 million between June 23 and and November 30, 1923. This was repeated at the end of World War II in Germany, Hungary, and many other states.

Due to the uncontrolled activities of banks, the current situation has become even more dangerous. In 1971, the dollar's convertibility to gold was ended and, in 1987, state oversight of the movement of capital was terminated. In the 1990s, this paved the way for financial speculation and toying with tax havens. Since the emission of bonds and other securities achieved global dimensions, the scale of economic and financial crises also grew. The last of these, the subprime lending crash (due to mortgage loans being made in the United States to people with limited ability to repay) shattered the foundations of the global monetary system and pushed the hevily indebted PIGS states (Portugal, Ireland, Greece, Spain) to the brink of financial collapse. To save the day, the US Federal Reserve began an unbridled emission of securities in 2008, during which the FED balance sheet tripled. The purpose of all this was to keep the economy going and to save the pension funds of the world's ruling financial elite as well as regular people pension funds from a significant write-off. At the end of 2008, the Federal Reserve emitted 16 quadrillion (10^{15}) US dollars, distributing it to the banks at 0% interest; another 800 billion (10^9) dollars was emitted by the Obama administration to help important manufacturing companies. This amount would cover Estonia's budget for the next billion years without any tax collection in the country. At the same time, the budget expenses of the US government were a mere 3,000 billion (10^{12}) dollars.

The European Central Bank (ECB) launched its bond-purchasing program in 2009, which continued at an even larger scale in 2012. Thanks to that, ECB's balance sheet increased by 25% and 75%, respectively! Although most of the last emission's bonds were redeemed by the end of 2015, the ECB initiated a new mandatory bond buy-up program that same year in order to stimulate the economy. This expanded even more in 2016, when the central banks of all member states had to buy up bonds for a total value of 80 billion euros. Dividing this amount by population of the eurozone, we see that 235 euros were emitted every month for every person. By the end of 2017, this totaled 10,000 euros per person in the eurozone! Thus, both ECB's balance sheet grew by three times from nothing.

Because borrowers paid the banks a tidy sum of interest for all these loans, it is small wonder that the wealth of the bankers grew at the speed of light, and banking became the most important means for concentration of capital. How this has affected the distribution of the wealth of society in the countries of the world can be found in the plentiful studies and analyses published by research institutes as well as state statistics offices. The reports of Oxfam International are particularly vivid.

Because the entire monetary system, especially paper money and electronic money, is based on **faith** and **trust**, we can only wait for the time that the people's faith in currency that is emitted to excess and lacks any coverage in goods will vanish. Nobody can predict when the next crisis will erupt and in what country but, based on previous experiences, we know that it will usher in an era of mass unrest and outbreaks of violence, and a time of profound social revolution. The cause of crisis is the unwillingness of people to forfeit their illusory wealth and agree to the release of "air" from the system as a condition for restarting the economy. If this were implemented in practice, it would mean that unsecured securities and debts for which the expectation of repayment is unrealistic, should be erased, and the rest should be reassessed to back them up with actual security. It would be much easier to transition to a new monetary system in which an identical amount, say, enough to cover two months' subsistence expenses, is distributed to all persons.

SPONTANEOUS ORDER AND MADE ORDER

In his essay "Cosmos and Taxis", Friedrich Hayek (1899–1992) compared the spontaneous order of market economy to the order created and managed by humans – i.e. the ruling elite. For this, Hayek adopted Greek words *"cosmos"*, meaning the spontaneous order of things and *"taxis"*, meaning the order directed by humans. Spontaneous order is a common object of study for physicists and biologists, but many of Hayek's contemporary economists refused to acknowledge the existence of this phenomenon. The study of this was not possible until after the emergence of cybernetics as a branch of science in the 1960s; however, its realization in practice had to await the birth of the virtual digital world at the end of the twentieth century.

Hayek stated that, despite the advances of science, humans are unable to create crystals or complex organic compounds by assembling them from individual atoms. However, scientists can indeed create the conditions in which these processes can occur, with the desired crystals developing by themselves in an environment modeled to include the proper conditions. We see countless such spontaneous processes in nature. As an illustrative example, he described how a magnet under a table will position all the iron filings atop a table into regular circles. Therefore – we are able to design environments and create the conditions in which the desired outcome will be achieved, but we can never determine exactly where each specific atom or iron filing should be positioned in this process.

The market economy is based on an analogous concept: we give people complete freedom to act and to engage in something for the purpose of improving their subsistence and well-being, with the condition that any harm resulting from their actions must be dealt with by the individuals themselves. Hayek found that although all people act for the purpose of pursuing their self-interest to the maximum (which continues to create conflicting situations), they also want to decrease risks (that arise from these conflicts), because that makes it possible to decrease costs, avoid losses, and ultimately earn more profit. Through trial and error, a person learns the following: cooperation that takes into account the interests of others, altruistic behavior, and economic relations based on trust are more advantageous in the long run than actions that are egoistic and focused on maximizing short-term profits.

All attempts to create a better society and greater well-being under the leadership of one great and wise ruler who know exactly what, when and how much each of his subjects should do, have been unsuccessful. Attempts to create totalitarian societies (based on hierarchical relationships of subordination) and planned economies have also ended in failure. From written sources, we know that the ruler Ur-Nammu (reigned from 2047 to 2030 B.C.) of the Sumerian Third Dynasty of Ur tried to create just this kind of social order in the latter part of the first individualistic civilization.

The Roman emperor Diocletian (245–313) and several rulers of the twentieth century, most notably Joseph Stalin (1878–1953), attempted to do the same. All these societies functioned very well at first, but later lost their position in stiff competition and vanished into the scrap heap of history. However, it is true that these periods were long recalled by some of the working masses as a "Golden Age".

In summary, there are few winners and many losers in a human-made order. In the planned-economy environment, the well-being of the common folk improves at first, thanks to redistribution of goods and profits, but this well-being turns them into passive consumers who ultimately no longer want to do or risk anything. When the previously created wealth runs out and the ruling powers no longer have anything to redistribute, universal shortages ensue, which sets everyone into competition for the remaining resources needed for survival. Increasing conflict and spreading violence ends in universal chaos and civil war that will not end if neighbors or other parties interested in the territory begin supporting sides in the conflict.

Still, Hayek supported limited intervention in market-economy processes by officials representing public interests to prevent the greater damage that could be caused by human greed for profit and short-sightedness, the epidemics brought about by war, and damage to the natural environment. He felt that human freedoms are not diminished if their actions are guided by laws that have been established and are known to all, and the officials who implement these laws do not act arbitrarily or out of self-interest.

THE FIELD OF ACTIVITY OF INDIVIDUALISM

In the two-dimensional model of social organization, the concept of "individualism" or "individualistic way of life" denotes one of four social orders, and its dominant features are

- the individual's aspiration to become free of the limits set by the community or state organization and to improve one's personal subsistence;
- the individual's desire to realize oneself, develop one's abilities and put them to the test in a competitive environment.

In the center of individualism as an egoistic way of life is the material sphere of life: ensuring subsistence, improving one's standard of living, and maximizing the capital that ensures well-being. The more skillfully the individual takes advantage of the freedom of self-realization and the opportunities offered by a market economy, the greater are the profits they will earn. However, if people increase their profits by harming other people or the physical and social environment, it will cause reactions that sooner or later begin to harm the individual's own property and existence.

Models of individualistic market economy are distinguished from each other by whether the purpose of economic activity is rapid accumulation of wealth or assurance of steady profit flow, and the degree of the individual's freedom of self-realization.

Market-Economy Models on the Axis of Equality

Figure 10. Individualism is based on market economy, but it has several forms. Moving from the center of the axis of equality to the right, i.e. toward the intensification of egoism, the models of social market economy > free market economy > capitalist market economy can be distinguished. By: P. Tammert.

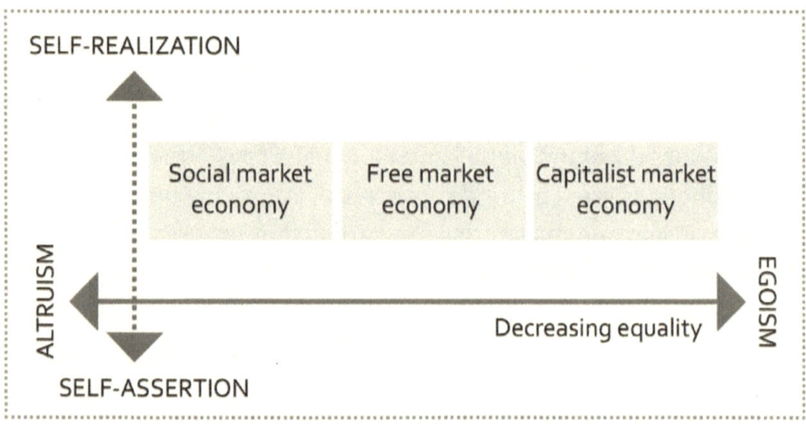

The axis of freedom of the individualism sector describes market-economy models that can be implemented in various cultural environments.

Social market economy is characterized by mutually beneficial cooperation for the purpose of ensuring the sustainability of enterpreneurs participating in the process at the state, company or individual level.

The goal of a **free market economy** is the realization of individual potential, thereby achieving the greatest possible profit from specialization and market economy. However, freedom that is based on self-interest amplifies inequality and polarizes society from within. With the development of global market economy, international competition intensifies and states must choose either to find trustworthy partners and make progress with cooperation, or to focus on self-interest and provoke a struggle for existence with other countries and cultures.

Capitalist market economy focuses on profit, and the supporters of the ideology of this economic model have no interest in what becomes of the workers, consumers, business partners and physical and social environment after the business transaction is completed or when one is no longer involved. All tricks are allowed, and nobody is going to judge the winners. At least, not people!

Concepts of Freedom

**Figure 11**. Individualism is based on the freedom of self-realization and the ideologies that represent it. Moving upward from the lower part of the axis of freedom denotes an increase in the number of people that have acquired the freedom of self-realization. As we move up from the center line in the individualism sector, there are the concept of negative freedom > the concepts of positive freedom > the concept of individualistic or anarchistic freedom. By: P. Tammert.

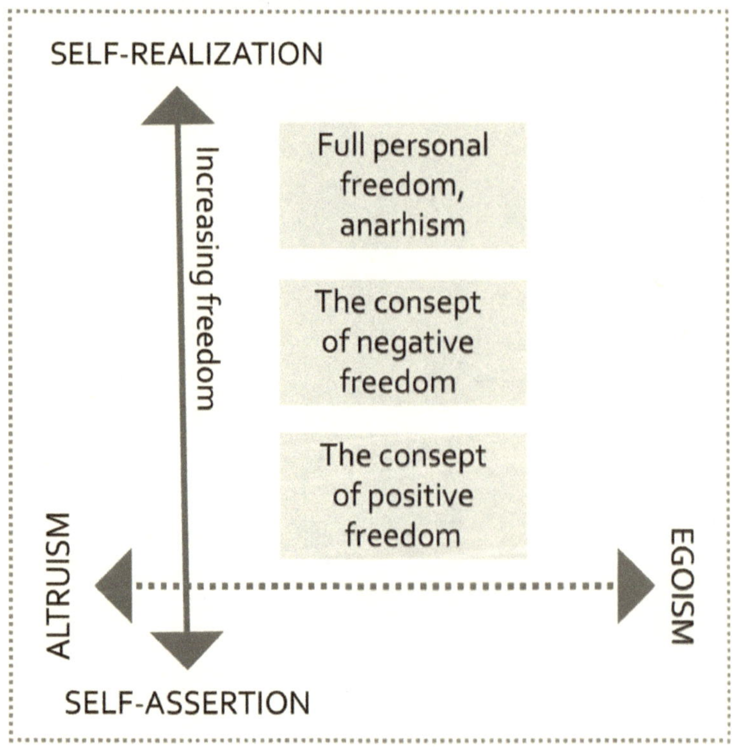

On the axis of freedom, the various forms of individualism are represented by concepts of liberalism, all of which are opposed to the paternalistic forces that limit the individual's freedom of self-realization. The oldest concept historically, that of **negative freedom**, emphasizes the individual's right of self-realization and opposes the privileges of the ruling elite (to be outside of the law, to avoid paying taxes, etc.) and the oppression that comes from the legislation imposed by the bureaucracy. The actions of individuals promoting the republican system of government as well as the liberal economic model and the movements that introduced these systems were based on this concept of liberty.

The historically newer concept of **positive freedom** was based on the international competitiveness aspect of society as a whole or the state. Because the strength of the whole depends on the strength of its parts, it became evident that the more society and the state contributed to the education and well-being of individuals, the stronger they grew in international competition. In everyday life, this meant that the state's competitiveness grew in proportion to the availability of education and the improvement of the level of teacher qualification, and the ability of public officials to keep the living environment clean and safe and to limit the activities of entrepreneurs who harm the living environment or social co-existence. However, achievement of this goal presumed limited redistribution of income in the form of voluntary donations or the payment of compulsory taxes to cover the operating costs of officials and to provide education for young people who are materially deprived but mentally capable.

Liberalism's extreme conception of promoting complete individual liberty is represented by the concept of **individualistic freedom** and **anarchist** ideologies that deny the need for the existence of state bureaucracy and official coercion. These ideologies feel that people can solve peacefully all their mutual problems themselves through negotiation, and that the danger of external interference only hurts this process. This may indeed be the case if all members of society have risen to such a level of erudition and tolerance that they can solve their problems by themselves and also engage in boycotting, through personal as well as economic relationships, those who violate the agreed-upon rules.

ELITARIANISM

Figure 12. Elitarianism is located at the lower left of the two-dimensional approach to social theory, i.e. it arises as the result of egoistic disposition and a behavior model that subjugates others. By: P. Tammert.

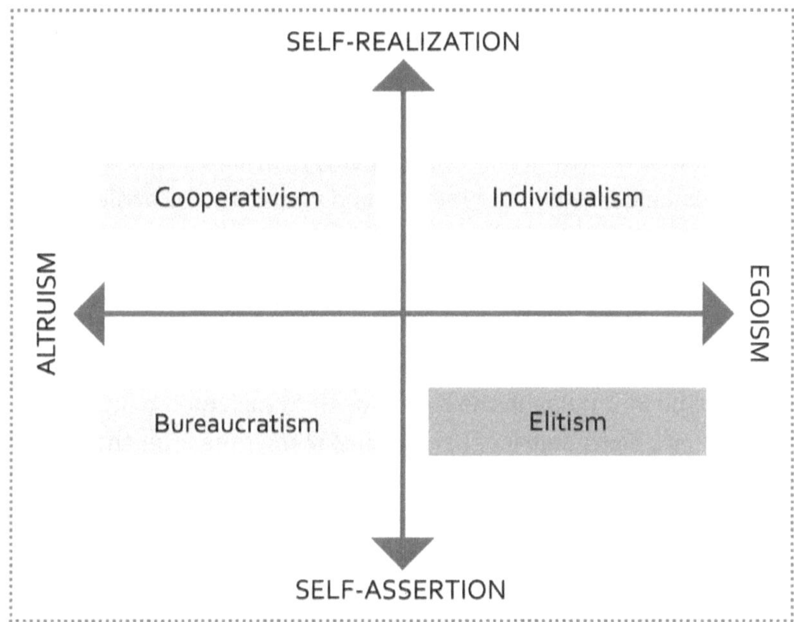

THE CONCEPT OF ELITARIANISM

For the purposes of this book, the elite are those people who rise to a level of personal development in the course of specialization (i.e. they achieve the ability to think independently, are able to understand the relationship between cause and effect and, based upon this, to imagine scenarios for future developments), but who, driven by egoism, choose the way of self-assertion. The school of thought that declares that some people are smarter than others, and therefore have the right to rule the land and people, is denoted with the term "elitarianism". According to this theory, the people have the "right" to listen to the advice of other potentates who are more worthy (wiser, wealthier) and are obligated to follow their orders. Historically, the ruling elite has included tribal elders, religious leaders and warlords who achieved their power by stirring up discord, dividing the community, and intensifying social conflicts.

The concept of elitarianism refers to a stratified class society organized by relationships of hierarchical subordination; these evidently came into being in the fourth or third millennium B.C. among the Indo-Germanic language tribes, some time after their separation from the Baltic tribes. All these vertically specialized tribes who descended from the tribe originating in the steppes of Russia are characterized by the existence of three orders: those who pray, those who fight, and those who work.

- Latin *oratores, bellatoeres, laboratores*;
- Indo-Iranian *brahmin/athravan, kshatriyas/rathaestar, vaishyas*;
- Greek (Attica) *eupatridae, geomori, demiurgi*;
- Greek (Sparta) *homoioi, perioeci, helots*;
- Roman *flamines, milites, quirites*;

- Celt *druides, equites, plebes*;
- Scandinavian *earl, churl, thrall*;
- Anglo-Saxon *gebedmen* (prayer-men), *fyrdmen* (army-men), *weorcmen* (workmen);
- Slavic *volkhvs, voin, krestyanin/smerd*.

Notable is the proportion of each group within each nation: the elite comprises only 2–3% of the population, the warrior class generally does not exceed 10–15%, and all the rest are workers who feed, supply, and guarantee the emergence of the next generation to secure the power of the first two groups.

The term "elitarianism" is used here to denote the human group passing on the right to rule through their blood line to their descendants; this right is based on their private ownership of capital and the social order that they represent. A communal tribal society becomes elitarian when the tribal elders take from their community, and warlords from foreign communities, the land that has been in common use and make it their private property that is then bequeathed to their descendants. Offering people many kinds of opportunities for subsistence, making them compete among themselves for the right to use capital and enjoy other benefits, and fanning the flames of envy allowed them to destroy the community social organization as well as the well-organized individualistic social organization. The implementation of the "divide and conquer" principle allowed a small but well-organized minority to secure its power over the multitudes and to make them serve the minority's interests and needs.

In this context, "elitarianism" denotes a social order based upon vertical specialization, concentration of capital and a social organization (state) that protects the privilege of capital owners and the injustice that arises from it. The driving force of both elitarian as well as individualistic social order is egoism, service of self-interest, and the desire to increase the amount of capital brought under one's power. Elitarianism differs from individualism in that it amasses capital without using market-economy methods, and by violating moral principles. The more glaringly and brutally they are violated, the more rapidly capital is concentrated, and the greater becomes the power of the elite.

SELF-ASSERTION AND POWER

The concept of "self-assertion", in this context, denotes the wish to force one's desires onto other people and to subjugate them to one's will, i.e. to limit or even eliminate their right to free self-realization.

The concept of "power" refers to the human ability to assert one's will and force others to submit. In interpersonal relationships, power is gained in circumstances where one person, by self-assertion, affects the thinking of another person to the extent that the other person submits to the asserter and begins to do something that serves the subjugator's interests. It is easiest to achieve this by sowing fear, fanning the flames of discord, and setting people into conflict with each other. Beset with a growing feeling of uncertainty, people start looking for protection from those who are stronger and smarter and can offer guardianship. It is significantly more difficult to create a situation in which people will agree to having the property they need for daily subsistence (land, money) go into private hands. This becomes possible only when the property that is the foundation of independent subsistence is taken away from the people and they become dependent on the owners of the capital. Such circumstances are achievable through the application of deception and mass violence.

Here, the source of power is private property and the organizational position to the property owner. Power is exercised through the unfair economic relations and the coercive measures applied by the unjust organization. Power is achieved when people who are born free submit to the will of another person and start to fulfill, either voluntarily or under coercion, obligations that are imposed on them, but are harmful to themselves. Power becomes absolute when people relinquish the right to think for themselves and no longer take responsibility for the consequences of their actions, i.e. they begin to blindly follow their leaders, hoping for their protectorship and grace.

One person may gain power over others by bringing them into his "food chain" and giving them a specific function with which they can ensure their everyday subsistence. Despite the reciprocal dependency, the power to make decisions still rests with the potentate, because only the powerful one knows how to keep the chain operating as a unit. In such a model of profit acquisition through division of labor, the lowest links in the chain do the "dirty work", and the highest enjoy the fruits of the labors of the other links in the chain.

When ruling families establish a lineage whose members are united by blood ties and the relationships that emerge from them, the system of power begins to expand and encompass larger groups of people (such as the Italian 'Ndrangheta). Family or clan relationships are generally passed along the male line. Such a family or clan evolves into a tribe with militaristic tendencies and, ultimately, tribal unions give rise to a nation whose members are united not only by origin, but also a common language and culture.

The power of warlords was ensured by their ability to organize and lead tribes or hordes comprising free men, who forced free people to submit to a foreign power's will by using or threatening force. The subjugation process started with the terrorizing of neighbors and demands of tribute payments (taxes) in exchange for a safe physical and social environment. The existence of a concentrated source of wealth helped fortify the warlord's power. This source might be mines containing a highly desirable natural resource (salt, precious stones, metals, etc.), or the right to use a valuable natural resource (water, forest, etc.), or an important trade route, for which a fee could be required to guarantee safe passage. The last and most difficult solution was the conquest of a populated territory and taxation of the population for funds to cover the expenses of their daily subsistence. Imposition of a permanent tax obligation presumed the existence of literate officials and the creation of a bureaucratic organization (military or premodern state). This required the warriors to surrender their absolute power.

Throughout history, **religious leaders** (initially shamans) have fulfilled the task of communicating with supernatural forces, shaping world view with explanations of incomprehensible phenomena, and offering solutions to personal health problems and conflicts within the community. When a religious organization based on the written word emerged, it took on the additional duty of keeping records, which paved the way for the emergence of a spiritual elite. The start of cooperation between these two elite groups introduced methods allowing the spiritual manipulation of the working population. A God was created in man's image. This God, with his all-seeing eye (symbol of the Freemasons), saw everyone and everything, and those who did not submit were threatened with God's wrath and the eternal torments of hell. This conception offered excellent opportunities to subjugate the working people without resorting to violence. When the financially successful (and therefore the most sinful) people also began believing the disseminated religious teachings, it forced them to make generous gifts to the religious organization to free themselves of sin and escape the torments of hell. In this way, religious leaders became managers of capital, and their influence in the state grew along with it. When religious leaders became the dominant force, the result was imposition of a theocratic form of government.

If the ruling elite succeeds in refraining from the imposition of overburdening tax obligations and the use of force, and can enact a moderate legal system, the military state can survive for a long time. Its character is determined by the kinds of practices used to keep public order and collect taxes. If this is done by warrior groups, a feudal state emerges, as was typical in the early Middle Ages of Europe. If keeping order and tax collection is delegated to local tribal elders or city councils comprising mostly wealthy merchants (who are interested in the existence of safe trade routes), a decentralized governmental structure develops, based upon cooperation between the elitarian social order and the community-based or individualistic social order.

If the ruling elite allows market-economy relationships to develop, the artisans and merchants, i.e. the bourgeoisie, become wealthier. With expansion of the market and advancements in production, the influence of the middle class grows accordingly, developing into a new, independent class. The groundwork for new developmental trends is laid when the wealth controlled by the richest segment of the middle class starts to exceed the wealth of the existing landowners and a money economy becomes dominant. The more adaptable members of the landed aristocracy retain their influence by creating an asset management enterprise that, in some states, is a form of charitable trust that allows avoidance of inheritance taxes ("trust" the Anglo-American legal space, "Foundation" in France and in continental European countries, "*Stiftung*" in Germany, "*bonyad*" in Iran, "*waqf*" in the Arabic legal space); the best business leaders are hired to manage them, and the revenues are distributed to the members of the family managing the fund according to circumstances and changing needs.

The emergence of the stock exchange business and public limited companies, and the growing influence of international trade that was wielded by the fund management companies controlling the capital, paved the way for the development of a bond market. Transition to paper money separated it from the physical foundation that itself once had value, and turned it into an independent form of capital. A new income-redistribution mechanism arose from the loan policies of the banks that were created to administer paper (later virtual) money; this mechanism is based on the right of private banks to emit loans (give credit without real money) and collect interest (in real money). This locks the borrower into inescapable debt relationships under long-term loan contracts and causes periodic liquidity crises. The power over capital starts to concentrate ever more rapidly into the hands of a small group of people, and this gives rise to a new kind of elite – financial oligarchs – who exercise power through monetary relations and thereby shape the development of all of society.

In a modern state wherever more people acquire a good education and value wise leaders, a new kind of non-hereditary elite called the meritocracy arises from among successful private business leaders and business-university professors. Their power derives from influence or authority (Latin *"auctoritas"* – "stature, influence"). There is no power of coercion, but the members of this group are able to influence the masses and direct them to act according to their wishes because of their positive example, charisma, capability and recognized knowledge. This manifests itself in the loyalty and willingness shown by people to faithfully and devotedly serve their role models and sources of inspiration.

In everyday usage, the peoples who support the nation's cultural identity are often referred to as the elite. Such a misleading use of the word should be avoided because the plenipotentiary power of the elite is based on the capital they possess or their authority over a state organization, and their skill at using this capital and authority determines their position in the social organization. In an elitarian society, those educated people who lack personal capital can only serve as advisors to the authorities; in the best-case scenario, they can influence the decisions of the rulers and thus also developments but can do so only indirectly by way of their knowledge and creativity. The words to better describe these people are "intellectuals" and "intelligentsia", thereby avoiding use of the misleading concept of "elite".

THE RULER

The person achieving power over a large number of people thanks to wisdom and competence is made their **ruler**. The Germanic tribes of the ancient and Middle Ages selected a king (Old Scandinavian *"konungr"*, Danish *"konge"*, German *"König"*, Low German *"könnig"*, Dutch *"koning"*, Norwegian *"konge"*, Swedish *"kung"*). If the king succeeded in bequeathing his power, he became a monarch (Greek *"μόναρχος, μόνος"* – "alone" – and *"αρχόςοn"* – "ruler"). The characteristics of a monarchy are the customs that have developed over a long period of time, implemented as general rules of behavior, royal court rituals, a system of reciprocal rights and obligations, etc.

If the person seeking power seizes it with deception or force, he becomes an autocrat. As a form of government, this is called autocracy. If the sovereign power is based on fear, the ruler is called tyrant (Greek *"τύραννος"*) or despot; in the Islamic cultural environment, caliph or sultan.

From the birth of the military state to modern times, marriage politics have been used as a means of expanding and securing power. Upon the marriage of people in authority, the marriage contract played a very important role, for it specified the rights and obligations of the parties at marriage as well as during the subsequent period when the power was actually exercised. The success or failure of such marriages has affected the fate of many nations and states throughout time, and has changed power relationships on the international level in completely unexpected ways. In contracting these marriages, the family tree, i.e. the ancestry of the candidate, played a very important role.

In 1865, Czech monk Gregor Johann Mendel (1822–1884) discovered the natural mechanism of heredity. English naturalist Charles Darwin (1809–1882) studied the phenomenon of natural selection and based his theory of evolution on it. Building on these theories, English psychologist Sir Francis Galton (1822–1911) suggested in his 1869 work *Hereditary Genius* that improvement of the human race can be achieved by joining wise men and wealthy women in marriage. This lay the foundation for eugenics (the science of improving the genetic quality of the race). Galton derived this term from the Greek "εὐγενής" ("well-born"). Through eugenics, it was hoped to promote human qualities that were generally considered to be good. These qualities included good health, vitality, adaptability, capability, courage and courtesy. The goal was to create a people who would be more reasonable, better able to concentrate, more farsighted, and politically more well-balanced. According to the theory, the more capable segment of the population was to be offered economic stimuli and services that would encourage their advancement and reproduction. At the same time, the number and reproductive capability of those less capable of improvement (people with mental handicaps, the incurably ill, those obsessed by unwholesome desires, etc.) was to be limited by restrictions on their freedom to travel and marry, sterilization, abortions, and other means. The teaching of improvement of the human race found many supporters throughout the world, particularly among politicians defending national culture who were concerned about their nation's state of health (organizations promoting temperance, healthy eating and exercise) as well as the preservation of their language (educational organizations).

The influence of the eugenicists was particularly strong in early twentieth century Western and Northern Europe, America and Japan, but the stock market crash of 1929 shattered the myth of the superiority of the elite, because many of them chose suicide, and a large segment of the former elite now stood next to representatives of the workers' class in soup kitchen lines. In Eastern Europe and the Baltics, including Estonia, the eugenics movement gained strength after World War I. The politics of racial cleansing and creation of an Aryan race developed farthest in Germany before and during World War II. Adolf Hitler (1889-1945) opined in his book *Mein Kampf* that the breeding of a disease-free race would take 600 years, but the genocide inflicted by the Germans against Jews and other non-Aryan peoples damaged the concept of eugenics to the point that the scientific world abandoned it completely. However, sterilization of handicapped people continued even after World War II in the Soviet Union, Czechoslovakia, Finland, Sweden, and several other countries until the end of the 1970s.

THE ELITE AND CLASS SOCIETY

When society is divided into two unequal groups – nobles and ordinary people – and an elitarian social order is put in place, only those with sufficient property for leisure are considered to be the elite. All the rest are "workhorses" whose subsistence and mode of living is arranged by the elite. Everyone must have one's own place in the food chain of the person exercising governmental power.

The concept of "class society" denotes a hierarchically organized society in which everyone's position is determined by their descent. There may be two or more classes. The first and most long-lasting class society is the Hindu caste system, which is also the most inflexible, because everyone's fate depends entirely on the caste into which they are born, and moving from one caste to another has been practically impossible. The caste system is in effect in many parts of today's India. In the Hindi regions, it is designated by the words *"jatis"* and *"quoms"*. It is present as a historical relic also in Nepal, Sri Lanka, Indonesia and Rwanda. In the Islamic areas of India, the caste system is denoted with the word *"biradari"*, it is dominant both in the Zaidiyyah community of Yemen and in Nigeria, Cameroon, and the Ivory Coast of Africa.

The class society in Ancient Greece, Rome, and Middle Ages Europe was not as inflexible, and moving from one class to another was possible, although not frequent. It was easiest to rise from the workers' class to the warrior class. Moving up into the higher noble class was possible with courage and leadership exhibited on the battlefield or with services rendered to the ruler; usually with a monetary loan that allowed one to purchase a title and position. Elimination from the higher class occurred mainly because of hedonism – surrendering oneself to pleasure, including gambling and the use of intoxicating substances, which resulted in the loss of the capital that was the foundation of one's power. Class status was lost less frequently due to betrayal of the ruler or failure to fulfill one's obligations. A milder class system predominates in western Africa, Gambia, Ghana, Guinea, Liberia, Senegal, and Sierra Leone, as well as Rwanda, Burundi and Somalia in Eastern Africa. In medieval Europe, the class system became most clearly delineated in France and Spain, where distinctions were drawn between the secular and religious elite.

At the end of the Middle Ages, a **class-based social order** developed in Europe, emerging from the individualistic progress of market economy and the growing wealth of the urban middle class, which became ever more influential for the ruler (tax revenues). A new, influential layer was now added to the existing class system — the urban bourgeois, who took the initiative in society and started driving economic progress forward, but who also became the main bearers of the tax burden. Apparently, that is the reason that the bourgeois was given the name of the "third estate" (_tiers état_) in France. The elite privileges were abolished as a rule, besides the social cataclysm caused by them: in France 1790, in Norway 1821, in Russia 1917, in Austria and Germany 1919, in Baltic countries 1920, in Hungary 1947.

The foundations for the existence of a class society vanished when the individualistic way of life, along with the bourgeoisie social order, achieved dominance in the economy, legislative power was transferred to a democratically elected parliament, and the hereditary elite lost the privileges it had been granted by the governing powers.

ELITARIANISM THEORETICIANS

Because elitarianism and class society are not natural orders of life, intellectuals in the service of rulers have time and again tried to create theories that justify the power of some people over others. Elitarianism is the opposite of the principle of human freedom and equality and regards democracy, national self-determination and the right to self-governance to be utopic visions that cannot possible be implemented in a mass society of stupid people. Nor can democracy and capitalism be compatible in the eyes of the elitarians, because the ability and skill to manage capital and manipulate the masses is given to only a few. Elitarianism is based on the idea that power proceeds from a person's ability to lead and to manage economic and political institutions.

Italian engineer, sociologist, economist and philosopher Vilfredo Pareto (1848–1923) believed that the characteristic of the elite was intellectual superiority, and that such people are the best in every field of life. Italian journalist, political scientist and official Gaetano Mosca (1858–1941) described the elite as a well-organized majority, and the common people as an unorganized mass. German sociologist Robert Michels (1876–1936) articulated the iron law of oligarchy, which states that only a specialized organization based on vertical division of labor, led by a few particularly capable individuals, can be successful. German–British sociologist, political scientist and philosopher Ralf Gustav Dahrendorf (Lord Dahrendorf) (1929–2009) claimed in his book *Reflections on the Revolution in Europe* that parties have become "service providers" that sell their visions of how to stimulate the national economy during the election campaign, and implement them when the votes they receive put them in power. Based on this conclusion, he proposed that political parties be registered as regular businesses that sell the service of executing public policy.

The influence of the elite on politics has been actively studied in the United States. Political scientist Elmer Eric Schattschneider (1892–1971) sharply criticized pluralistic theories and claimed that policy in a democratic society is actually shaped by the most educated and highest-income individuals, and the masses are left out of this process. Sociologist Charles Wright Mills (1916–1962) claimed in his book *The Power Elite* that actual state power has fallen into the hands of narrow and self-interested groups of politicians, capitalists and officials, thanks to attempts to make processes more rational and effective. Sociologist and official Floyd Hunter (1912–1992) studied power relationships at the local level and, in *Regional City*, he described the hierarchical power relationships between local businessmen, politicians and officials. Sociologist and psychologist George William Domhoff (born 1936) continued Hunter's work, analyzing the local and national decision process in his *Who Rules America?* and drawing the conclusion that American politics are actually determined by a small elite that runs the international companies and banks. In his book *The Managerial Revolution*, philosopher and political scientist James Burnham (1905–1987) claimed that leaders of large businesses have the most influence on the content of policies, since capitalists and politicians do not participate in actual economic processes. Political scientist Thomas R. Dye (1935) stated in *Top Down Policymaking*, as well as in later works, that public policy is not based on "the will of the people", but on the consensus of the ruling elite, and is shaped by the non-profits, think tanks, special interest groups and legal offices that lobby in Washington D.C. Based on his investigations, political scientist Robert David Putnam (born 1941) concluded that it is the administrative specialists with strong knowledge in the special fields of management as well as psychology who have acquired the most influential position in the political decision-making process. Political scientist George A. Gonzalez (born 1966), describes in *Corporate Power and the Environment* the formation of environmental and energy policies and the elite's role in it. Economist Martin Giles and political scientist Benjamin I. Page (born 1939) analyzed the decision-making process of 1779 political decisions and came to the conclusion that nearly all the decisions were made based upon the interests of the business elite, and the people's public interests could not prevent their adoption.

THE FIELD OF ACTIVITY OF ELITARIANISM

Elitarianism as a form of social order emerges and persists with the combination of two forces, whereby its driving forces are

- **an economic model that deepens inequality** and redistributes profit and wealth, or an organization of society that deprives individuals and nations of their property and subjugates them in order to possess the fruits of their labors;
- **freedom-limiting organizations** that protect the privileges of the elite who are in the minority but rule the majority and create systems that contribute to the subjugation of the masses and the railroading of the activities of these masses to achieve certain ends.

The elitarian social system becomes dominant when communities and individuals who, until this point, have recognized individual freedoms relinquish their freedoms and submit to the will of those attempting to achieve supremacy, due to fear and pressure from unfair economic relationships. If the people begin to blindly follow their rulers and surrender their right of independent thinking or lose it altogether, the road is open to the supremacy of the minority, and the foundations of democratic organization of society are lost.

Methods of Securing Inequality on the Axis of Equality

Figure 13. Elitarianism is based on the economic model that serves egoistic greed for profit or the form of social organization that concentrates all property into the hands of a small ruling elite, finally rendering all the rest of the people propertyless. By: P. Tammert.

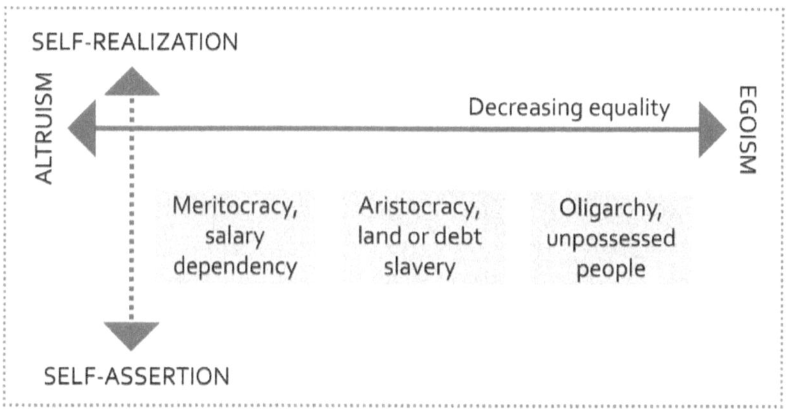

The segments of the elitarian sector's axis of (in)equality are distinguished from each other by the nature of the ruling elite and the extent of the people's poverty.

The salary dependence is the mildest form of elitarianism in which a constantly changing, mutually competing, advancing class of capable people (the meritocracy) is ruling through the capital ownership. In this model of elitarianism, people are essentially free, but economically dependent on their employers. Dependency is created with a combination of small salaries and high cost of living or high consumer prices.

The debt bondage-based society, ruled by the aristocracy is significantly harsher and more unjust because all capital (sources of subsistence) has been concentrated into the hands of the hereditary elite (the aristocracy). In this economic model, people are bound by ground rent or monetary debt interest such that they are locked into debt, never to be free of it. Although they are essentially free people, their debt relationship binds them to the owner of the capital and, essentially, they become an accessory of the capital they are allowed to use. By entering a creditor–debtor relationship, people lose the right to make their own decisions, and are forced to serve the owner of the capital for as long as they have not paid what they owe on the loan.

Without private ownership life is harsh and society is ruled by oligarchs. Here, people have lost all their material property. Because propertyless people are completely dependent on the grace of their masters, employers or benefactors, they have no say about their personal affairs or the work obligations that have been imposed on them; they have also lost any right to express any opinion or to participate in the decision-making process for society.

Methods of Self-Assertion on the Axis of Freedom

The segments of the axis representing the limiting of freedom are distinguished by the method with which individual freedoms are restricted.

Economic subjugation is the system, limits itself to capital-based relationships, whereby these are distinguished by the method and extent of the exploitation.

Mental subjugation of the people implements religious organizations and world-view teachings that inject the fear of God's all-seeing eye and the torments of hell into the human conscience; the disobedient will be the ones to suffer. The communication between human and Creator is monopolized and declared to be the exclusive right of the organization's representatives (clergy). They also monopolize administration of justice as well as the right to dominate the people's mental world; here, the confessional plays a significant role.

Physical force and the fear of death are the final measures, that is implemented to squelch any human desire for freedom and to subjugate the population is. If even this is not enough, the vanquishers still have the earthly property that once belonged to the murdered people and the tribes and nations they have destroyed.

Figure 14. Elitarianism achieves its goal by implementing measures that consistently limit individual freedom of self-realization; they are: economic measures > spiritual measures (religion) > physical force. By: P. Tammert.

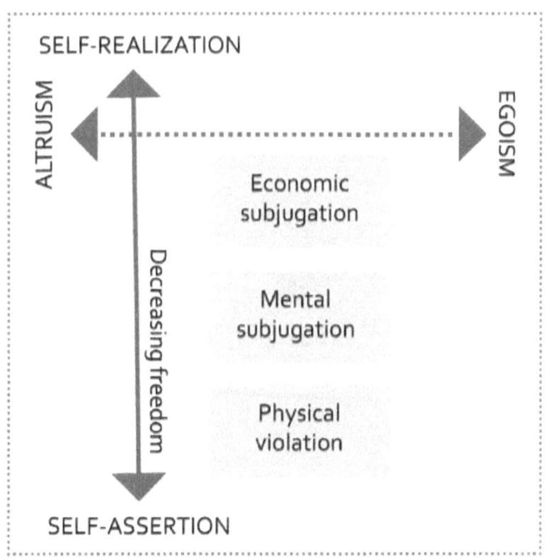

BUREAUCRATISM

Figure 15. Bureaucratism is located at the lower left of the two-dimensional approach to social theory, meaning that it is established by altruistically-thinking government officials (who base their actions of the interests of society as a whole), who at least initially try to improve the sustainability of the state institution. By: P. Tammert.

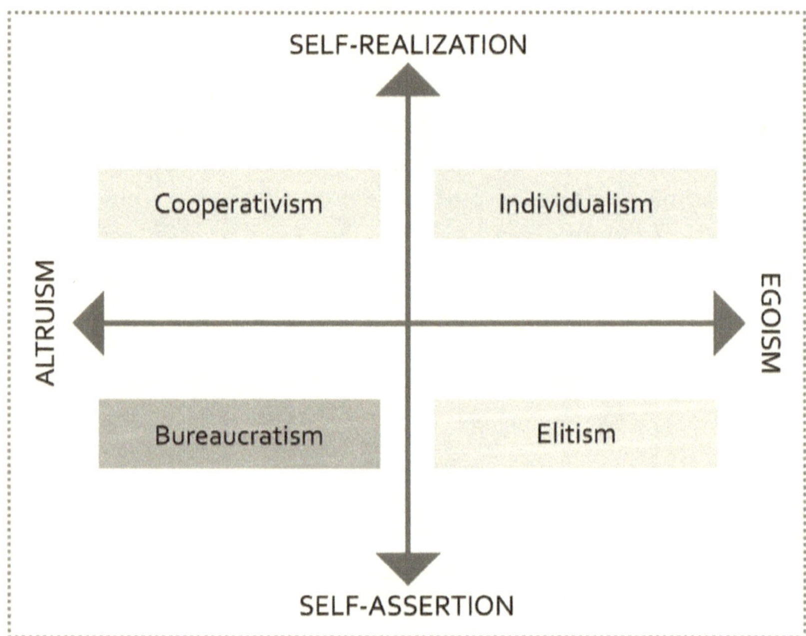

THE DEFINITION OF BUREAUCRATISM

The bureaucrat (official, public administrator) is a specialty that emerged in the environment of the individualistic social order. The groundwork for this was laid by people who had achieved a high level of personality development, who could overcome the egoistic way of thinking budding from within themselves, and whose vision of the future surpassed their personal perspective. Looking at society as an entity and perceiving the dangers originating from competition among societies, they understood the role of altruism in ensuring the sustainability of society. The profession of "official" was born of impartial administrators of justice who, in a market-economy society, began administering justice to people who were blinded by greed for profit and engaging in mutual conflict because of it.

The concept of "bureaucratism" refers to an organization of society that is based on specialization and organized by the state, where officials exercising executive power standardize the legal order of society based on its own interests. The role of official as the representative of public interests evolved in an individualistic market-economy environment. Along with it, there developed a territory with common legal order that got the name of "state". "Practice" for society is the same as "habit" for an individual. A practice adopted by a society becomes tradition; bureaucratic institutions – departments, ministries, and inspectorates – emerge from collective customs, as does the form of government. Bureaucratism becomes the determining force for society when professional officials start directing the development of society by writing laws and bringing the legislative body (parliament) under its power.

Etymologically, the first part of the word "bureaucracy" comes from the French *"bureau"*, meaning a felt-type cloth covering for a writing desk. The second half of the word means power, and the concept as a whole refers to rule by officials. As a political science term denoting ideology, it is given the suffix -ism, resulting in "bureaucratism".

Bureaucratism began to develop after the birth of the state institution, because the city-state, comprising artisans and merchants, needed to ensure order in their market-economy relations. Because officials had to be impartial and represent the common interests of society, the society had to provide them with a permanent income and an agreed level of well-being. Later their activities expanded to include executive power.

According to prevailing practice, oversight of adherence to laws and regulations, administration of justice, and punishment of violators of the law have been the responsibility of the state bureaucracy. The success of bureaucratic order depends on whether society is willing to recognize and abide by the rules laid down by the bureaucracy. Those legislative acts that are intelligibly written, provide good protection for the established legal system, and solve social problems effectively, are quickly accepted. A legal system that increases or entrenches injustice and hampers the customary way of life can be enforced only with coercive power, i.e. in cooperation with representatives of elitarian governing authorities.

When officials start managing the progress of society and dictating the behavior of individuals based on their own interests, bureaucratism becomes the dominant force in the state. It is often not possible to ascertain who is doing the leading and what is being sought. Signs of the strengthening of a bureaucratic organization of society are:

- social, public discussions are transferred to closed committees;
- a new law is enacted to solve every social problem;
- limits are placed on enterprise, which is subjugated to official interests through the issuing of licenses;
- activities of the individual are regulated, and a steadily growing system of oversight is created to monitor adherence to regulations;
- the obligation to compensate for damage caused by crime is replaced with the practice of punishing criminals with imprisonment and having them supported by the income of bureaucratic organizations;
- the overall tax burden becomes ever greater to cover the expenses of the bureaucratic organization.

Bureaucratism, like the militaristic organizations from which the bureaucratic organization arose in the form of Prussian cameralism, is characterized by a clear hierarchical structure, impersonal relations, standardized ritualistic procedures and a clear division of labor. The concept of "civil service" is indicative of its militaristic origins while clearly emphasizing that it is a non-military service. It should be noted here that, before the beginning of the Christian era, in China evolved inside the paternalistic culture, influenced from Tao's philosophy, Buddhist religion and Confucius teachings, a civil bureaucracy that played an important role in ensuring the sustainability of the government system and the people.

In the opinion of German jurist and philosopher Max Weber (1864–1920), the bureaucratic leadership model is appropriate for organizations that are large and significant from the standpoint of the state (army, police, ministries, local governments, railways, etc.) specifically because of its clear divisions, standardized order of communication, and external controllability. The effect of bureaucracy on the advancement of society and the state was particularly positive at the start of the modern age, during the era of industrialization, dominance of big businesses, and mass production. In a social state, bureaucratism ends up being a progress-inhibiting force, because its desire to standardize, regulate and subjugate everything to universal control will hamper the development of an economy and society that is becoming ever more diverse.

Social inequality and injustice deepen in a society with a dominant extreme capitalist form of individualism or elitarianism (monopolism or totalitarianism). The resulting tensions may give rise to violent revolution initiated by the suppressed and exploited masses or lay the foundation for an intertribal civil war. Only a bureaucratic system of government is able to prevent these developments and lessen tensions in the society. Bureaucratism's main tactic is the promise it makes to the public to restore order and restrict inequality (not injustice!) through redistribution of wealth. In return, the state's subjects are required to voluntarily submit to the prescribed order and not interfere in negotiations with the individuals who manage the capital. Because negotiating and execution of agreements are different actions by nature, and presume the existence of different intellectual skills, the profession of politician and official are thus distinguished. Politicians and officials, paid by the state, start fulfilling the role that was previously played by the hereditary elite.

POVERTY

Although the problem of daily subsistence has been topical throughout time, no agreement has been reached on its unambiguous, fully understandable definition of poverty. In natural-economy communities, a person's subsistence depends above all on the presence of land and the person's own diligence. In a market-economy environment based on specialization, a person's economic position depends on how successful one is in selling one's labors or in exchanging the fruits of one's labors. If the capitalist mentality becomes dominant, and if inequitable economic relationships become the norm and exploitation intensifies, the number of people who cannot support themselves will grow. The problem of poverty is worsened and entrenched by an elitarian form of government that uses deception and force to take away the fruits of people's labors and the property they need to subsist and forces them to work for pay that will ensure only minimal subsistence. In a market-economy society, a person is considered impoverished if 60% or more of their income is spent on food.

Poverty can be defined in various ways, depending on whether the problem is approached from the point of view of the person or of society. If the point of departure is the person, the following degrees of poverty can be distinguished.

- **Absolute poverty** means inability to obtain the resources needed for living – clean drinking water, food, clothing, shelter and medical care. Temporary absolute poverty can occur as a result of a natural disaster or climate change, including crop failure, that leaves people without food, clean drinking water and ultimately, a place to live. Permanent absolute poverty is brought about by unfair economic relationships that take from people their land and other sources of subsistence, but more rarely a person's own reluctance to work and improve one's competitiveness, or inability to make progress and adapt to a changing environment.

- **Relative poverty** is a concept that is called actual poverty in modern states. It refers to people earning significantly less income than the median, meaning those who are unable to consume as much as others. Relative poverty has always existed, and it appears in every market-economy society in which the quality of a person's life is rated by their capacity to consume. The Nobel laureate of Bengali descent, Indian–English–American economist and philosopher <u>Amartya Kumar Sen</u> (born 1933) has defined such poverty as a "deprivation of basic capabilities of self-realization and social benefits".

Looking at poverty from the standpoint of a modern state, two distinct causes can be discerned.

- **Subjective poverty** arises from unwillingness to work, or to offer up one's physical or intellectual strength in order to obtain something. This model of behavior is rooted in the family; it becomes evident in school as inability to exert oneself intellectually, and later continues as inability to work in order to cover one's subsistence expenses. It sounds paradoxical, but the subjective poor are often the most egoistic and greedy of all; they want a lot, but are unwilling to give anything in return. They are the people who rush to sales, trampling others under their feet, and are always the first to arrive whenever something is being handed out for free. The subjective poor can be recognized by their loud lamentations about the injustice that is prevalent in society. This segment of the population is derisively called "human garbage", and the society that pities these people and demands "equal rights of consumption" for them is destined to fail.

- **Objective poverty** can strike people who lose their parents and grow up as orphans, become incapacitated due to accident or illness, lose their ability to work because of old age, are unable, as single parents, to cover subsistence expenses, and other reasons. Objective poverty can arise also from an unjust system of government in which most of the population lacks the opportunity to obtain education and live in a healthy manner; these are the most important conditions for successful subsistence. Such people are truly in need, and their opportunities to improve the situation are limited or nonexistent. If the world wants to be humane, it will try to help these people as much as materially possible. However, from the standpoint of long-term progress, the way in which the needy are helped is important – by distributing money and improving opportunities for consumption or offering training and subsistence opportunities that allow people to find their own path and a personally suitable way of self-realization.

By offering everyone equal opportunities for education and allowing selection of a subsistence model that is personally suitable, impoverishment can be more effectively contained. However, how much people are willing to educate themselves depends on the people themselves, and how they realize themselves depends on their willingness to apply will power. The task of the bureaucratic organization is to ensure educational opportunities for all and to keep the physical and social environment in a condition that allows everyone to live a healthy life, and to limit unfair economic relationships and crime, using budgetary resources from tax revenues and the coercive force of the state.

EGALITARIANISM

The concept of "egalitarianism" ("equalitarianism", "equalism") derives from the French words *"égal"* ('equality') and *"égalitaire"* ('equalizing, directed at equality'). As a political concept with the suffix -ism, it denotes the policy of equalization.

Egalitarianism is a philosophical as well as sociopolitical theory that seeks answers to questions related to equality and equalization in human society. In any case, egalitarian ideology expands along with the strengthening of bureaucratic authority, because officials are unable or unwilling to consider all the differences originating from lifestyle or environmental factors. It is much easier to prepare regulations and registries and keep records on the presumption that all units being recorded are identical.

Bureaucratism becomes an independent organization of society and achieves a dominant position when the hereditary elite is removed from power and an association of professional officials and politicians emerges along with the emergence of a democratic social order. In a total-democracy society where the dependency mentality predominates, the responsibility-free life offered by this association enjoys tremendous support. This lifestyle is promised to the subjects in exchange for their willingness not to intervene in the activities of the authorities. In the process of social specialization, bureaucratism bears the responsibility for the subsistence of the community and the sustainability of society, leaving the people with only the right to "demand well-being". A majority of the population cannot resist such an appealing proposition and, by agreeing to this, they pave the way for the supreme authority of the officials as well as an egalitarianist (wealth-redistributing) policy.

The weakness of the bureaucratic order is that fact that the bureaucrats themselves produce nothing. The bureaucratic organization can only redistribute

- the products that come into being in an ever more efficient individualistic market-economy environment, along with the income they generate;
- the property – i.e. capital – that is the foundation of subsistence and economic activities and which the elite who represent the capitalist mentality have brought under their control.

If the representatives of the bureaucratic system of government succeed in redistributing the capital that is in the hands of the elite in a way that provides a maximum number of people with opportunities for subsistence and improved well-being, the bureaucracy will be successful, at least for some time. However, by intervening in manufacturing activities and intensively redistributing manufacturing income, the stimulus to continue engaging in the manufacturing process is taken away from the people who are capable of maintaining and improving the process. This will cause the source of revenue providing the flow of wealth that the bureaucracy is redistributing to dry up. It will weaken the plenipotentiary power of the officials' organization and ultimately cause its downfall. All attempts to appeal to philanthropy, i.e. the idea of selflessly helping the needy, will fail, because people no longer think of helping others when their own opportunities for subsistence have been destroyed.

Moral egalitarianism defends the standpoint that all people are equal at the moment of their birth. The resultant conception of human rights states that all people have identical intrinsic basic rights, independent of sex, race, religious convictions or citizenship. This principle was internationally recognized with the Universal Declaration of Human Rights that was adopted by the United

Nations in 1948. The most direct opposite of egalitarianism is elitarianism, which considers inequality, the privilege of the minority, and discrimination based on origin, race, language or religious convictions to be natural.

Legal egalitarianism is based on the presumption that society is made up of individuals, and the opinions of all members of society should be taken into account when making decisions that affect the society. In principle, all persons are equal before the law (the concept of a state based on rule of law). Whether the laws actually help to increase equality is largely dependent on whether these people use their rights. The principle of individual equality was first set forth in the Bill of Rights, passed in 1689 by the Parliament of England; its legality was confirmed by the joint sovereigns William and Mary.

During the French Revolution, under the banner of "Liberty, equality, fraternity", the Declaration of the Rights of Man and of the Citizen ("Déclaration des droits de l'homme et du citoyen") passed and adopted by the National Constituent Assembly in 1789, established equal rights for all male citizens (French "l'homme"), but left out the women ("la femme")! The 1776 Declaration of Independence of the United States of America adhered to the same principle, based on the custom of gender differentiation that is characteristic of Indo-European languages. Some delegates, the most renowned being the representative from Pennsylvania, John Dickinson (1732–1808), refused to sign it, demanding that the word "men" be replaced by the word "person". Despite that, use of discriminative words continued in the text of the American Constitution of 1787.

Economic egalitarianism promotes the principle that all people should have equal opportunity to ensure subsistence for oneself and one's family. Chinese thinker Xu Xing found as early as 315 B.C. that according to the principle of justice, the same goods should have the same price everywhere and at all times, despite differences in their production costs and quality, and the market supply-and-demand relationship. Throughout time, opponents of capitalism and private property have demanded equality of land use (the foundation of community way of life). After the advent of the Industrial Revolution, some demanded to have the added value being amassed from specialized manufacturing and business profits divided among participants in the process. Here it should be noted that Karl Marx never demanded the equal distribution of capital or profits among the workers.

Social egalitarianism is an outgrowth of economic egalitarianism; it demands equality in consumption. This demand was presented by American philosopher and political activist Thomas Paine (1737–1809) in his 1795 work *Agrarian Justice*. Because of the unprecedented jump in productivity and the concurrent deepening of inequality, the twentieth century saw a search for means of fairer distribution of manufacturing profits and improvement of consumption opportunities for the poorer segment of the population. Even some of the capitalists realized that manufacturing would lose its value if consumers had no money to purchase the goods. The bureaucratism that was establishing a society of well-being tried to solve the problem by increasing the tax burden and expanding the social welfare system. In societies with individualistic market economy, the idea of "basic or citizen's income" took root; economist Milton Friedman (1912–2006) developed this further at the end of the twentieth century with his concept of negative taxation.

However, in the 1990s it became clear that state budgets – due to the free movement of capital and "tax havens" that offered services allowing tax avoidance – would be unable to cover the necessary costs of welfare services in the globalizing economic environment. It also became clear that a system seeking equalization of consumption would not be sustainable, because an ever-greater segment of the population was indeed wishing to consume, but not participate in the production process. The use of natural or energy shares and their equal distribution among all persons was offered as a new solution. The substance of this proposal was that the replenishable natural resources or energy potential should be divided by the number of people and used as a unit of money in market-economy relationships. However, the flaw in this solution is the danger that a system that redistributes only replenishable natural resources would not encourage people to participate in production.

Religious egalitarianism in the form of charity is typical of many religious organizations, but it is usually limited to trying to increase equality only among the members of one's own faith, and calls on people more or less publicly to exploit all those of a different faith or the faithless. An exception is found in the teachings of Sikhism, which demands universal and all-encompassing equality, independent of sex, faith and race.

In summary, we can say that, in simple terms, egalitarianism means striving for universal and total equality, which is actually not possible to achieve, because

- people are born with different genetic heritage; their willpower, ability to work, and orientation to material and spiritual values differ a great deal;
- a person's opportunities for self-realization are strongly affected by family background and circle of friends, as well as the material opportunities, social contacts, and other factors originating from them;
- different physical and social environments offer differing opportunities for subsistence and self-realization;
- people's wants and needs and ways of self-realization are different, and their level of intellectual development

amplifies this inequality even more, to an undetermined degree.

Egalitarian policy hampers a person's ability and willingness to exert oneself when seeking economic well-being. And yet, we can boldly claim that inequality will not grow to unnatural excess if officials are capable administrators with the skills to maintain the legal order that proceeds from public interests and entrenches fair economic relations in a democratically-governed state. However, any attempt to increase redistribution of wealth and establish complete equality will regress into populism and end up as a dictatorship enforced by the bureau of officials.

OFFICIALS AND THEIR POWER

The concept of "official" denotes a worker serving the ruler or government, exercising executive power and fulfilling official duties in an office. Officials may be salaried or receive payment and resources needed for subsistence from their management of a specific source of revenue or the collection of resources. The role of the official was born in an ancient society based on individualistic division of labor. At first, officials represented the temple that was the institution promoting the society and economic relationships of the city-state.

The institution of officialdom developed from the role of the long-ago tribal chief of a community society and the judge in an individualistic society. Its influence began growing rapidly in the individualistic city-state in which the official, in addition to resolving domestic and economic disputes between people, had to also start organizing market relationships. With greater specialization and development of statehood, the number of officials also increased, creating a bureaucratic organization that was tasked not only to dispense justice, but to administer the public space and organize national relations.

The class society that was characteristic of ancient Egypt was based on a vertical division of labor, in which officials, as scribes, held an extremely important position, because without tax registries and property records, the entire system would have collapsed. In Sumeria, the ancient Egyptian kingdoms, and the Chinese empire, officials were educated in temple schools, and many of them became wealthy in their position as high officials. Much information about their social activities and duties has been found in Egyptian tombs. Even more information about the work of officials has been gleaned from Mesopotamian clay tablets.

The institution of officialdom spread by way of the Greek and Roman temple culture to medieval Europe, where these duties were carried out by the clergy of the Roman Catholic church organization. Canon Law began using the Latin word "_officialis_" ("official") to denote a clergyman (vicar) with judicial authority in service to the bishop; this person resolved civil disputes and was the leader and shepherd of his congregation.

The official's main duty has been the recording of events and information, the archiving of the collected data, and oversight of performance of the duties assigned to subjects of the state and the members of the organization. Throughout history, the duties of the bureaucratic organization have included the collection of gifts, donations, and tax revenues, keeping accounts of payments received, and organization of the distribution and use of existing funds. In elitarianist societies, they were also expected to write and keep chronicles. The role of the secular official developed as an outcome of the power struggle over tax revenues between the secular ruler (the king) and the bishops representing the ecclesiastic organization. The concept of "official" in the singular first appeared in a chronicle of 1314 England, after the establishment of an organization comprising people in service to the king and secular officials. At first, the role of official was the privilege of the ruling elite, but in the era of the Commonwealth of England from 1649 to 1660, it transferred to the middle class and became a salaried job that was paid from the tax revenues collected into the state budget.

A **secular governmental authority** that managed all facets of state life by way of militarily organized ministries was created in Prussia after the Protestant Revolution of the eighteenth century, during the rule of Friedrich Wilhelm I (1713–1740). It was during his era that people would speak of "an army with its own country". And this – initially the poorest of the German states – ultimately united all the principalities into one German nation.

In his works, German sociologist and jurist Max Weber (1864–1920) has studied the role of officials and the bureaucratic organization in detail. To summarize his studies, officials are defined as persons

- who must communicate with the subjects of the nation in the officially recognized national language;
- who are personally free, and are appointed to their post by the person executing the pertinent administrative power;
- who must be impartial in their work and sacrifice personal interests if these interests should come into conflict with their official duties;
- who operate on the basis of impersonal authority granted by law;
- who are loyal in their acts to the person bearing governmental power;
- whose specific post and career depend on their competence;
- whose administrative work is a full-time occupation;

- whose work is rewarded by a regular salary and prospects of advancement in a lifetime career;
- who are guaranteed an old-age pension at the end of their career.

The influence of the bureaucracy began to increase when the large European territorial states came into being. In the modern state, officials held the important role of market regulators. Not until the social state did officials become a dominant force. The plenipotentiary power of the bureaucracy depends on the mentality of society. As the demand for redistribution of wealth and proprietary equality grows, the power of officials becomes more extensive and all-encompassing.

Power refers to the capacity of an individual to influence the conduct of others according to one's wishes. There is a power relationship inherent in every human relationship and any kind of intragroup behavior. The influence of an individual is evident in their talent to convince others to do what that individual wants, and these skills arise from that individual's personal qualities and social status. Along with a position in the state hierarchy, the official acquires the power of office, i.e. authority – the right to require people to abide by a certain model of behavior or to do something they otherwise would not do, all with the threat of government enforcement. The word "authority", denoting stature or influence, is derived from the Latin "*auctoritas*"; its German-language synonym is "*Herrschaft*", which denotes nobility and gentry, but also government and power.

Max Weber distinguished three types of power arising from authority:

- the legitimacy of rational-legal authority derives from the legal order and laws of a territorial state; the obligation to obey them is secured by a state-level apparatus of enforcement;

- traditional authority is based on cultural traditions and ingrained practices, and is passed from one generation to the next (such as the hereditary right to rule or a hereditary office);
- charismatic authority derives from personal attributes; it is backed up by a collective group mind ("_egregore_"); therefore, it is also often referred to as "power conferred by God".

In today's bureaucracy, the organizational team (i.e. officialdom) believes, for the most part, in the legality of the enacted rules, and thus in the right of the person assigned the position of leadership to give orders. In exchange for their work, the officials receive a salary, the size of which depends on their position in the hierarchy, and which should motivate them to carry out the tasks that are assigned to them. Because the bureaucratic organization of society is based on division of labor, and officials are assigned to their posts on the basis of competency rather than personal loyalty, this kind of state organization has proved to be the most effective means of executing state power.

THE FIELD OF ACTIVITY OF BUREAUCRATISM

Bureaucratism, as a specific form of social order, arises from the combination of two forces, with the driving forces being

- **an equalizing (egalitarian) policy** that is used to justify redistribution of material wealth and financial equality to increase the social capital and sustainability of society as a national whole;
- **a method of limiting freedom** that is based upon the presumption that individuals will relinquish their freedoms

to the bureaucratic organization and its representative officials in exchange for its guardianship.

The particular form of bureaucratism and the field of activity of its governmental culture is determined by the method that is chosen to limit freedoms and the concept that is chosen for increasing equality.

Policies that Increase Equality

Figure 16. Egalitarian policies deepen and the (consumption) equality of people increases as we move leftward from the center on the axis of equality. The model of the egalitarian organization of society is represented by policies of a well-being policies > welfare policies > ideological equality policies. By: P. Tammert.

The forms of bureaucratism are distinguished in the sector of the axis of equality by the extent of redistribution of income and wealth.

Welfare politics is historically the oldest one; it came into being in England after King Henry VIII (1491–1547) abolished the

Catholic Church organization and disbanded all the convents and monasteries that had administered welfare. His daughter Elizabeth I (1533–1603) was forced to enact laws that imposed the obligation to care for its needy onto the communities, which established the Working houses. States with Calvinist religion also established networks of social welfare institutions staffed by people with specific duties.

Well-being politics is the mildest one, based to the humanist ideology. This policy was introduced by the Social Democratic parties in the end of twentieth century and implemented in many Northern and Western European states. To govern the society here is possible to use

Egalitarian politics is based on ideology, which aims for absolut equality and unification. This may be manifested in seeking equality of consumer rights, or denying differences proceeds from the gender and genetic heritage (feminists), or in demands return to the original subsistence village economy (dark greens). It may be manifested both through the ecclesiastic judge's ruling society, basing their administration of justice on a word-for-word interpretation of sacred texts (the case of Islamic states etc.). The most extreme form of egalitarianism is communism, under which all capital and private enterprises will be nationalized and managed by state and party officials (bureaucrats) on the principle of a planned economy.

Methods of Limiting Freedom

Figure 17. Policies of the bureaucratist social order in order of
increasing coercion: fiscal policy > legal policy > terror policy. By:
P. Tammert.

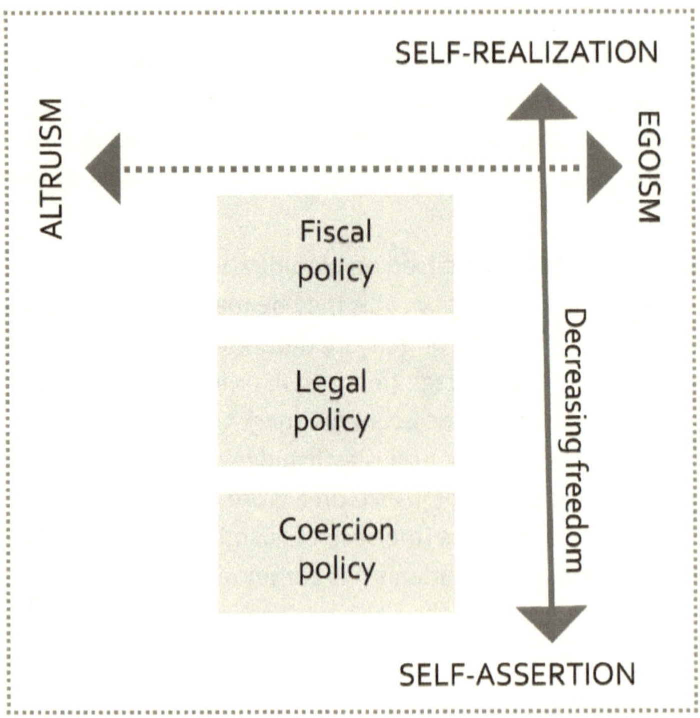

The segments of the axis of freedom are distinguished by the
field of paternalistic policy that is used to limit individual freedoms.

Fiscal policy is the mildest method, which uses taxation
(general consumption tax, custom tax, excise duty) to make
undesirable things and behaviors less profitable (progressive

income tax), and uses monetary support from the state budget to make desirable activities more profitable.

Legal policy is harsher, and thus more freedom-limiting, which contributes to legislative limitations, greater oversight, and increased severity of punishments in the form of forced labor or imprisonment.

Coercive policy is the extreme method of limiting freedom with force so that it generates fear. Terror is always directed at the people of one's own state and applied by an organization representing the bureaucracy interests (KGB, Gestapo, Stasi, etc.).

THE MATRIX OF IDEOLOGIES

<u>Figure 18</u>. The matrix of ideologies. The matrix of ideologies summarizes the previous presentation and places major political ideologies into the two-dimensional model of social order. The content of these ideologies is not the object of discussed here, as a good reader will find desirable clarifications from the Wikipedia, if there isn't another and better source. By: P. Tammert.

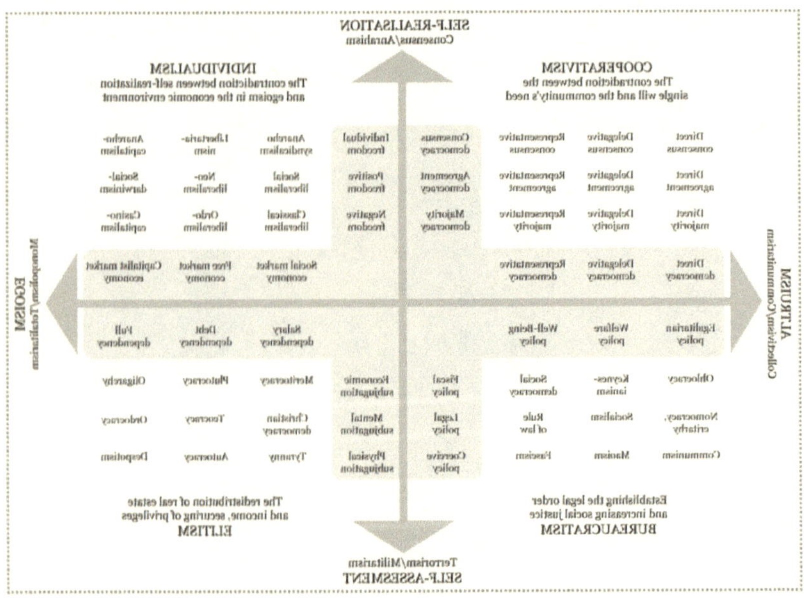

Look for better picture: https://p2pkoolitus.ee/ideologies/

THE THIRD AXIS

Figure 19. In the three-dimensional approach to social theory, the two current axes (equality and freedom) are joined by a third axis – fraternity – which is, by nature, a non-physical phenomenon, and takes the approach to human development as well as social problems to the level of the spiritual world. The driving emotions of the brotherhood axis are divine (spiritual) love and material evil. By: P. Tammert.

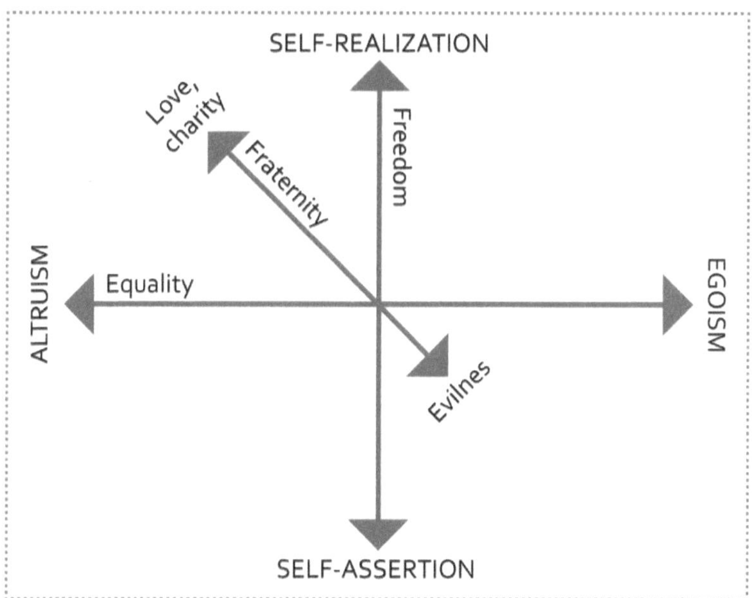

A TIME OF REVOLUTIONARY CHANGES

The human race on planet Earth has reached a truly critical time at the start of the twenty-first century A.D., because so many fundamental changes are taking place at once. The human population has grown so large that it has started harming the natural progress of Nature. The entire current geologic era has been given the name "Anthropocene". The consumer society springing from egoism, led by people who are driven by greed, values only the size of profit and is burying the world in garbage. It is unclear whether the warming of the climate is caused by human activity, or is the result on some greater cycle during which the atmospheric temperature, CO_2 content and amount of particulate matter undergo periodic change. Looking at the referenced diagram we see that the climate was warming for a very short time and rapid cooling and an ice age followed. So, human guilt might be that we postponed the beginning of a new ice age. However, even that is uncertain, because cosmological studies have shown that the Solar System has entered an interstellar cloud (Local Bubble) left behind by a supernova that exploded here long ago; although it is quite sparse, it is still significantly warmer than the surrounding environment.

Figure 20. The temperature, CO_2 content and particular matter in the atmosphere of the planet change in periodic cycles, with the duration of one cycle being about 120,000 years. The research is based on data obtained from deep drilling of the ice at the Antarctic research station at Vostok. Because atmospheric temperature and CO_2 content had become equally as high 120,000, 240,000 and 330,000 years ago, it would be hard to believe that human activity was to blame during these periods. In viewing this diagram, one might begin to think that the causes of

176

these periodic changes should be sought from the cosmos. And if we must blame humankind for something, it would be only that the temperature has not dropped as it did the last times, but has remained higher. Source: Wikipedia, Climate change.

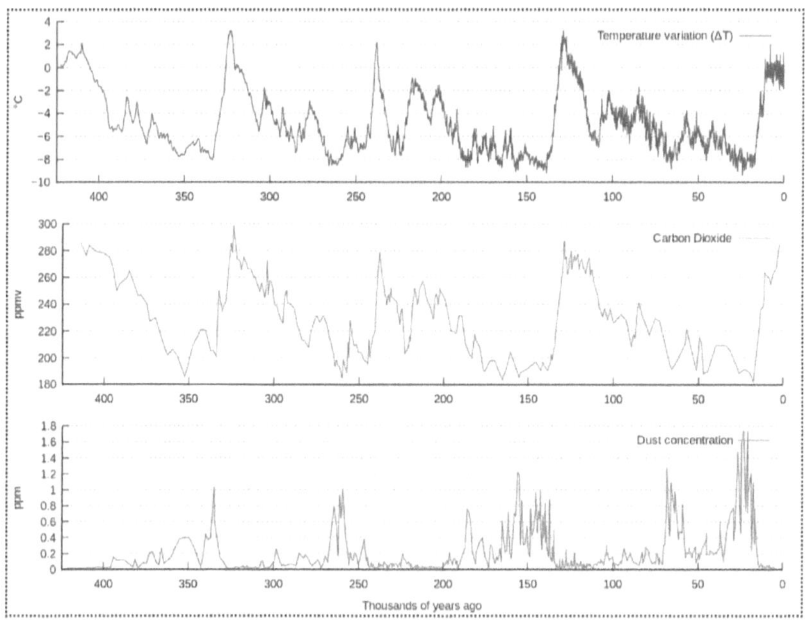

An even greater danger for humankind is the depletion of vital resources and the risk of their disappearance. The authors of the book *Limits of Growth*, which lay the foundation for the Club of Rome, described future scenarios for humankind. This book, initially published in 1972, was later repeatedly revised, and the predictions for the future presented in its 2017 edition state that dramatic changes will begin in the 2020s, lasting until the end of the century and resulting in a dramatic decrease of the human population. In the worst case, this means an era of great migrations and wars; in the best case, an 80-year economic decline caused by the diminishing of markets. This process will begin with the collapse of the monetary system due to loss of trust, because an assessment completed as early as 2009 claimed that 85% of securities had no cover. The process may be set into motion by an economic crisis that will be started by the trade war initiated by the intemperate president of the United States Donald Trump (born 1946) or the debt crisis of some large economic state (Italy, China or the United States). The scale of these revolutionary events will be amplified by unfair (capitalist) economic policies, as a result of which a majority of securities have been concentrated into the hands of 1% of the Earth's population.

Additionally, we are entering a severe cultural crisis brought about by technological progress, more precisely the Fourth Industrial Revolution. It is being caused by the replacement of the current alphabet-based method of recording and exchanging information with exchange and preservation of information that is based on pictures and speech, an outgrowth of digital information processing. In comparison, we can look at an analogous breakthrough that occurred in the first century B.C., when the cuneiform-based Mesopotamian culture perished and was replaced by the recording of information based on the Phoenician alphabet, which we use until this day. At that time, it triggered 400 years of chaos in the region that had been the world's engine for development and it is a developmentally backward region until today. Could this be the case with Western society, as the development of oriental culture based on pictorial writing becomes the driver of development?

Yet another crisis is rising from the deepening of a materialistic world view and the decline of religions that have been maintaining legal order in one way or another. Today, most of humankind is convinced that the universe is limited to that part of the cosmos that is composed of atomic matter (actually comprising

4% of the mass of the universe). The rest of the universe (about 21% dark mass and 75% dark energy) has remained a mystery to mankind and its leading scientists.

Moreover, there exists a notion that violates the law of conservation of energy, claiming that no other (read: spiritual) world exists. This means that the nature of human personality emerges from a nothing and dissolves into nothingness, and a person's earthly existence is a unique and never-repeated event. Because materialistic science is unable to ascertain the nature of the universe outside the atomic world or to prove its existence, and has therefore set about denying its existence, the foundation of yet another crisis has been established. By claiming that human earthly life is invaluable, and that people lack the right to decide how long they want to remain on this planet, we have created a true hell for ourselves, with the fear of death (actually fear of losing subsistence security) playing a determining role. Based on their materialistic world view, representatives of the capitalist and paternalist ideology claim that a person is a subject given to them, and they can do with people what they want, and that people themselves do not have the right to oppose their will. Humanists (an ideology that is materialistic from its conception) are convinced that since human life is of supreme value, people have no right to commit suicide or request euthanasia if all the opportunities offered to them by this physical life have been exhausted. Thanks to the selfless work of medicine, we now have an ever-increasing number of disabled people (many of whom with behavior more reminiscent of immobile plants or emotion-expressing animals) and elderly, to whose care we are devoting an ever-increasing proportion of society's funds. Thus, we have paved the way for one more crisis, caused by an increasing demand for welfare resources, while people who are able to support themselves refuse to contribute anything to the resources that are required (i.e. they are unwilling to have their tax burden increased or make their own charitable contribution to the support of family members).

Based on the theory of social order described above, we can state that one developmental cycle has been completed. This cycle started with the natural-economy community and developed through specialization into individualism, elitarianism and bureaucratism. The innovation that was born of specialization and enjoyed progress in a free economic environment expanded the developmental borders of a society that had achieved self-realization in this material environment. However, it seems that we are drawing ever closer to these borders. And, therefore, we must ask: where to, now?

THE THIRD DIMENSION OF THE APPROACH TO SOCIAL THEORY

In 2010, physicist Dejan Stojkovic and his colleagues at the university at Buffalo attempted to create computer models of the process of the creation of the universe, and they discovered a primeval weirdness, according to which the Big Bang that gave birth to our universe was followed by one-dimensional progress, as a straight line. Not until later did the second dimension (plane) arise and, even later, a third dimension (the space we live in today). Thanks to the expansive growth of space, the temperature dropped, the formation of matter began, and gravitational forces developed. This model also gave rise to an interesting prediction – our three-dimensional space has expanded to such a great degree that it will cause the emergence of a fourth dimension! British cosmologist Stephen Hawking (1942–2018) went even farther than the Buffalo physicists in his book *The Universe in a Nutshell*, in which he introduces an 11-dimensional (*sic!*) universe where superstrings constitute entire universes.

In describing the development of human society on the basis of social order and the forms of development of statehood, we can perceive multidimensional progress. In the material world (two-dimensional scale), the process of development was set into motion by specialization and the resulting ability to produce ever more and higher-quality products from the same amount of raw material. The surplus that emerged due to increase in productivity, and the wealth it generated, put (and continues to put) people to the test, bringing to light the qualities of their personality and the latent essence in the depths of their soul.

The approach to society being described here is unique because it proceeds from the person and the person's development. Specialization and the resulting individualization opened the way to personality development, on which every person who had attained a high level of personality development had to choose a path of self-realization or self-assertion. A new era of development for humankind began in the third millennium B.C.; in the process, the human mind separated from the universal subconscious (to use the concept presented in Ken Wilber's book *Up from Eden*), and the development of the personalistic person began. Many religions call this separation "original sin".

Development of a personalistic, egoistic temperament can be best observed in the course of the development of a child's self-awareness, which culminates in puberty. We can observe similar developments in the progress of human societies during the 4,000-year era following separation. Here, a determining role was played by the people who first reached a high level of personality development, who chose the path of self-assertion and subjugation of others (thereby paving the way for an elitarianist social order) and neglected to use the opportunity to contribute to the development of society as a whole. Therefore, in the one-dimensional approach, we can call all those people and ideologies (but only with respect to their time and place) leftists or reformers; they were the ones who tried to reshape society to allow the enhancement of freedom of self-realization for those people who had entered their path to personalistic development in a market-economy environment. In the societies that passed through the modernistic system of government and achieved the developmental level of a social state, all the ideologies that realized their program (republicans, liberals, socialists, communists and social democrats) have become the conservatives, because they want to halt the process of development and take society back to the times in which their own ideology was the progressive one.

The author of this work proceeds from the notion that the idea of human existence is the personalistic development, and the goal of this existence is the experience that one achieves through the innovative activity. In this context, the two-dimensional approach described above has exhausted itself because, within the limits of purely materialistic development, it is no longer possible to show any new social order that would support personalistic development or the paths to progress that proceed from it. Therefore, a third dimension must be added to the current model. Since development started with a cooperativist social order, and the vector of development progresses in a spiral fashion, the new social order, when the cycle is complete, should the based on cooperativism, but it should be implemented on a new level from which it will continue to progress.

Liberty, Equality, Fraternity

The phrase "Liberté, égalité, fraternité" was adopted as the official slogan of the First Republic during the French Revolution in 1789 at the suggestion of Marquis de Lafayette (1757–1834) and the decision of the Estates General. The initial proposal included a fourth word as well ("Liberty, equality, fraternity or death"), but the last word was ultimately omitted because it was derived from the revolutionary slogan "Live free or die". Because the government of Maximilien de Robespierre (1758–1794) justified its total terror with the idea of "There is no freedom for the enemies of freedom" and brought in the use of the guillotine to implement this policy, modern French society is extremely pained at the thought of any limits to freedom of personalistic development.

In the French Declaration of the Rights of Man and of the Citizen of 1789, the essence of liberty, freedom and fraternity were explained as follows.

- **Liberty** meant the opportunity to do anything that does not harm the rights of others.

- The concept of **equality** opposed the privileges of the elite above all, especially the right to not pay taxes. The principle of equality set forth that all people are equal before the law, i.e. all people, independent of their origins, have an equal obligation to society!

- The essence of the concept of **fraternity** was explained in the section dealing with the rights and obligations of citizens in the third constitution of 1795 as *follows: "Do not do to another that which you do not wish should be done to you; do continually for others the good that you would wish to receive from them." Because the post-revolutionary empire and kingdom refused to recognize this slogan, they* *did not become the official catchwords until 1880, after proclamation of the French Third Republic.*

Article I of the Universal Declaration of Human Rights, adopted by the United Nations in 1948, states:

*All human beings are born free and equal in dignity and right. They are endowed with reason and conscience and should act towards one another in a **spirit of fraternity**.*

Following France's example, India added this motto to its constitution in 1950. The Danish Social Democratic Party has also used these three words as their identifier. The statutes of the Liberal Democratic Party of Great Britain establish the party's basic values as being liberty, freedom and community, with these words printed onto the membership card of every member. The German national anthem includes the words "unity, justice and freedom" (*"Einigkeit und Recht und Freiheit"*). The German Social Democrats have interpreted this as follows: "Liberty is freedom from degrading dependencies, and the opportunity to develop freely within the confines of the requirements justice and solidarity ... Justice stands for freedom of the individual, giving him equal rights and comparable opportunities in society ... Solidarity expresses the experience and insight that we may live together as free and equal human beings only when we feel responsible for each other and help each other. For us, solidarity has a universal human significance; hence, it may not end at national boundaries."

Many of the philosophers who have pondered the development of society and agonized over the survival of humankind have opined that, in today's world, these principles have been implemented in part, and in only a few fields. If we apply these opinions to social order theory, the ideas might be summarized like this:

- Representatives of individualistic market economy demand **freedom** of enterprise, to which representatives of the capitalist orientation add the demand to freely seek profit and the right to amass wealth without limits … even if the activities are based on deception and force, and start to damage the subsistence and survival of the entire community or society.

- The bureaucratic social state seeks to **equalize** people's income with the taxation and social welfare system, to standardize people's knowledge through the educational system, without considering each person's actual abilities and interests, and their individual need for self-realization.

- The supporters of elitarian government culture demand **fraternity** and glorify the collectivistic organization of society. This means vertical division of labor, i.e. some do the work so that others can lead and rule them. The elite should be released from tax obligations and legal responsibility, because when one's actions are based upon public interests, something could go wrong, and part of society might suffer because of it, although "they meant well". The problem with this kind of "fraternity" is inherent in the fact that the elite, in order to achieve its goal, must manage administration of justice, which renders it impossible to recognize the unfair economic relationships that make up the foundation of the elitarianist governing culture and to limit the ensuing injustice. The result: those members of the elite (one's own) who have gone overboard with their profit greed are declared innocent in the courts, and those outside the circle are found guilty, thanks to the advantages of the elite privilege.

The Austrian philosopher, social reformer and esotericist Rudolf Steiner (1861–1925) founded the philosophy of anthroposophy, offering his own solution to replace this merciless organization of society, in which

- **liberty** should reign supreme in the spiritual sphere, i.e. everyone should have the right and freedom to study and improve oneself as much as possible according to one's abilities and wishes, to thus engage in self-realization and be beneficial to society;
- **equality** should reign in the legal system, i.e. all people are equal before the law, regardless of their family origins, circle of friends, and membership in organizations;
- **fraternity** should reign in the economic sphere, i.e. the idea of economic activity is to satisfy people's vital everyday needs and ensure the subsistence of society as a whole.

The history of humankind up to this time has clearly shown that it is practically impossible to root the idea of interpersonal fraternity in a society based solely on a materialistic world view.

The Dimension of Fraternity

In the physical world, fraternity is limited to blood-fraternity, based in the truest sense of the word on blood relationships (family, tribe), blood spilled in common struggle, or the ritual symbolizing blood sacrifice.

However, the phenomenon of fraternity can be viewed from the aspect of transcendental psychology, the essence of which is particularly well summarized by Ken Wilber in *Up from Eden*. In primitive communities in the natural-economy phase of development, the person was a part of the magic subconscious of the conscious universe. Before a person becomes a personality, the person must be conscious of oneself as an independent, autonomous subject and acquire knowledge to an extent that allows one to independently distinguish between good and bad, to learn to see paths of progress opening up before them, together with the influences they exert on the person themselves as well as the environment around them.

By separating from the magical subconscious, the person setting out on the road to personalistic development has entered the long and difficult road to self-realization, at the end of which one becomes an independent personality. This process is well described by the statement "Only the young and the dead fish swim with the stream!" Starting out on the road to personalistic development implies independent thinking, the constant checking of the suitability of conventional culture and common truths in a changing physical and social environment and choosing between "good" and "bad." The personality no longer wishes to submit to the will of the ruling authorities. The person begins a struggle to free oneself from the subjugating authority and seeks sovereignty in making decisions affecting one's life. The issue of justice rises to the forefront of the person's focus.

These days, the process begins in puberty, when young people resist their parents' rules, want to make the decisions for their own life, and learn about real life and its limits through personal experience provided by mistakes. Only after passing through this stage of resistance does a person begin to seek opportunities for cooperation with like-minded companions and other personalities. This lays the foundation for interpersonalistic cooperation and communal activities and teaches the person to be tolerant of other personalities by becoming aware of their motivations. Evidence of achieving this developmental level is present when the person's focus turns to love, mercy and service to others.

A new stage on the road to personalistic development begins when a person becomes conscious of oneself as a created, eternal spiritual being and starts to reflect over existential issues. This opens the way to the understanding of principles of truth, beauty and goodness that rule in the spiritual world. Perceiving oneself to be an eternal but constantly evolving personality in the divine spiritual world, a person acquires the opportunity to overcome the limits of the material world and become aware of the immortality of personality. The hallmarks of the evolutionary process of the whole personality is that he begins to see the truth, beauty, and goodness that governs our universe. According to Wilber's concept, the human spirit, upon attaining the level of harmonic personality, comes into union with universal superconsciousness as an independent being, signifying the transfer of the experiences acquired during one's development to one's Creator.

Another source that explains the nature and structure of a universe unknown to materialistic science in detail is the _Urantia Book_. This has been called the Fifth Revelation that members of the spiritual world have given to humankind; it was recorded between 1924 and 1955 in the United States (author unknown). The book is divided into four parts.

- *Part I, titled "The Central and Superuniverses," addresses what the authors consider the highest levels of creation, including the eternal and infinite "Universal Father," his Trinity associates, and the "Isle of Paradise."*
- *Part II, "The Local Universe," describes the origin, administration, and personalities of the local universe of "Nebadon." the part of the cosmos where Earth resides. It presents narratives on the inhabitants of local universes and their work as it is coordinated with a scheme of spiritual ascension and progression of different orders of beings, including humans, angels, and others.*
- Part III, "The History of Urantia," compiles a broad history of the Earth, presenting a purported explanation

188

of the origin, evolution, and destiny of the world and its inhabitants. Topics include Adam and Eve, Melchizedek, essays on the concept of the Thought Adjuster, "Religion in Human Experience," and "Personality Survival." *This section also gives an example of social organization on one another planet.*

- *Part IV, "The Life and Teachings of Jesus," is the largest part at 775 pages, and is often noted as the most accessible[34] and most impressive,[35] narrating a detailed biography of Jesus that includes his childhood, teenage years, family life, and public ministry, as well as the events that led to his crucifixion, death, and resurrection. Its papers continue about appearances after he rose, Pentecost and, finally, "The Faith of Jesus."*

The *Urantia Book* comprises 196 papers (about 2,000 pages, 6.2 million characters), and each one is attested by spiritual beings from various spheres of the spiritual world. As the author of this book, I must add that the contents of the *Urantia Book* overlap to a significant degree, as regards our known universe, with the results of investigations by members of the scientific world view community, but also talks about states of matter and phenomena unfamiliar to our scientific world. Referring to the *Urantia Book* in this context is justified, because it is the only source that provides a satisfactory explanation of the idea of fraternity and the role of love in our world, while also explaining their influence on the development of the person.

The *Urantia Book* describes **fraternity** as constituting a fact of relationship between personalistic beings in universal existence. The Creator and the fraternity of the personalities, He has created represent a paradox of the part and the whole. The nature of fraternity will become comprehensible to humans when they recognize the spiritual dimension and their personal relationship with the Creator God. According to the *Urantia Book*, the Creator gave humans, as created developmental creatures, complete freedom of self-realization; but along with this came personal moral responsibility for the consequences of one's actions. People cannot grasp the nature of fraternity until they become conscious of the existence of the spiritual world and recognize the personal relationship between themselves and their Creator. A personal and direct relationship with the Creator is the universe reality to all moral creatures, because everyone who has been bestowed personality is encircuited within the grasp of the universal personality circuit. The personality worships God first, because He is, then, because He is in us (through the mediation of Thought Adjusters) and, last, because we are in Him. Because fraternity is universal, it constitutes a fact of relationship between every personality, not only in the relationship between human beings and the Creator. Fraternity is a reality of the total and therefore discloses qualities of the whole in contradistincion to people limiting themselves to the reality of the material world.

No person can escape the benefits or the penalties that may come as a result of relationship to other persons. The individual enjoys well-being and suffers along with the whole (family, nation, state, planet Earth, the universe). The good effort of each person benefits all people; the error or evil of each person augments the tribulation of all people. As moves the part, so moves the whole. The relative velocities of part and whole depend on cosmic fraternity. Nobody can take without giving in return. On the path of personalistic development, the person first learns to be loyal to the whole, then to love, then to become conscious of one's inheritance deriving from the Creator and the ensuing relationship, and only then achieves a state of total freedom that manifests in the disappearance of the limitations of material existence. A person

cannot enjoy complete freedom of self-realization until that person
has become aware of the rules enacted by the Creator, and
recognized and adopted them, or has begun to act in accordance
with them.

The mortal consciousness of the created being proceeds from
the act, to the meaning, and then to the value. Creator
consciousness proceeds from the thought-value, through the word-
meaning, to the fact of action. Heredity originates from the
Universal Creator, and from this arises universal fraternity –
between all personalities in the universe.

Love

The feelings that set the axis of fraternity in motion are love
and evil. In typical speech, the word "love" denotes the relationship
of affection between two people. The Ancient Greek philosopher
Plato distinguished between three types of love: *eros* (erotic love),
filia (brotherly love) and *agape* (divine love). The word *amore*
(romantic love) derived from the Latin word *amō*.

In the Chinese materialistic world view, the Confucian word
ren was predominant, signifying benevolent love that was focused
on human relationships and was related to family and clan
structures. The philosopher Mozi (about 470–391 B.C.) attempted
to bring the concept of universal love into Chinese culture and
expand the concept to apply to all people. Also, in ancient Japanese
culture the concept of love was associated basically with human
relationships, and particularly with motherly love. In Indian culture,
love was associated first and foremost with sexual relationships, but
later expanded to include the emotional state brought about by
cultural phenomena. The same could be said about the pre-Islamic
Persian cultural environment. According to the Islamic world view,

love unites all believers, and the source of all-encompassing love is God: Al-Wadud. According to Sufi teachings, love is the divine form of being that humans perceive in their heart.

Love was central in Early Christian teachings. In the Bible's Gospels of Matthew and Mark, Jesus taught them that one should love God with all one's heart, mind, and soul, and that one should love one's neighbors as oneself. In Paul's First Epistle to the Corinthians, he states emphatically:

Love is patient, love is kind. It does not envy, it does not boast, it is not proud. It does not dishonor others, it is not self-seeking, it is not easily angered, it keeps no record of wrongs. Love does not delight in evil but rejoices with the truth. It always protects, always trusts, always hopes, always perseveres. Love never fails. And now these three remain: faith, hope and love. But the greatest of these is love.

The *Urantia Book* discusses the topic of love in the most depth, with the word "love" appearing 674 times. In comparison, the word "freedom" is used only 259 times. According to the *Book*, love is "**the desire to do good to others**". Love is the essence of religion and the wellspring of superior civilization. However, a religion that seeks love by fanning the flames of fear is like an economy that serves its members by amassing profit. The message of the *Urantia Book* for twentieth-century humankind was and is: it is time to break free from the selfish egoism that has been the driving force of many nations up to now. It is true that the rebellion initiated by Lucifer in the spiritual world has helped spur these developments; because of this, planet Earth along with many other fellow sufferers have been isolated from the source of divine love.

Despite all this, every person has the freedom to turn, in one's mind and with the mediation of a Thought Adjuster, to one's Creator, the one who has given them the seed of personality. For a person limited to material reality, *Truth*, *Beauty* and *Goodness* mean the full realization of divine reality. By adhering to the fundamental principles of the Universe, every person can enjoy the fruits of divine love: intellectual peace, social progress, moral satisfaction, spiritual joy, and cosmic wisdom. In the true meaning of the word, **love** connotes **mutual regard of whole personalities, regardless of their nature and level of development**. Truth is a liberating revelation, but love is the supreme relationship in spiritual reality. The ultimate goal of human progress is the achievement of brotherhood of man and the opening of oneself to divine love.

Here are a few excerpts from the first papers in the *Urantia Book*:

> *'God is love'; therefore his only personal attitude towards the affairs of the universe is always a reaction of divine affection. The Father loves us sufficiently to bestow his life upon us. 'He makes his sun to rise on the evil and on the good and sends rain on the just and on the unjust.' … God's love is by nature a fatherly affection; therefore does he sometimes "chasten us for our own profit, that we may be partakers of his holiness." … But the love of God is an intelligent and far-seeing parental affection. The divine love functions in unified association with divine wisdom and all other infinite characteristics of the perfect nature of the Universal Father. God is love, but love is not God. … At times I am almost pained to be compelled to portray the divine affection of the heavenly Father for his universe children. This term, even though it does connote man's highest concept of the mortal relations of respect and devotion, is so frequently designative of so much of human relationship that is wholly ignoble and utterly unfit to be known by ay word which is also used to indicate the matchless affection of the living God for his universe creatures … When man loses sight of the love of a personal God, the kingdom of God becomes merely the kingdom*

of good. Notwithstanding the infinite unity of the divine nature, love is the dominant characteristic of all God's personal dealings with his creatures. (Paper 2:5:1–12)

Righteousness implies that God is the source of the moral law of the universe. Truth exhibits God as a revealer, as a teacher. But love gives and craves affection, seeks understanding fellowship such as exists between parent and child. Righteousness may be the divine thought, but love is a father's attitude. The erroneous supposition that the righteousness of God was irreconcilable with the selfless love of the heavenly Father, presupposed absence of unity in the nature of Deity and led directly to the elaboration of the atonement doctrine, which is a philosophic assault upon both the unity and the free-willness of God. ... Facing the world of personality, God is discovered to be a loving person; facing the spiritual world, he is a personal love; in religious experience he is both. Love identifies the volitional will of God. The goodness of God rests at the bottom of the divine free-willness—the universal tendency to love, show mercy, manifest patience, and minister forgiveness. (Paper 2:6:5, 9)

The religious challenge of this age is to those farseeing and forward-looking men and women of spiritual insight who will dare to construct a new and appealing philosophy of living out of the enlarged and exquisitely integrated modern concepts of cosmic truth, universe beauty, and divine goodness. Such a new and righteous vision of morality will attract all that is good in the mind of man and challenge that which is best in the human soul. Truth, beauty, and goodness are divine realities, and as man ascends the scale of spiritual living, these supreme qualities of the Eternal become increasingly co-ordinated and unified in God, who is love. ... Truth is coherent, beauty attractive, goodness stabilizing. And when these values of that which is real are co-ordinated in personality experience, the result is a high order of love conditioned by wisdom and qualified by loyalty. The real purpose of all universe education is to effect the better

*co-ordination of the isolated child of the worlds with the larger
realities of his expanding experience. Reality is finite on the
human level, infinite and eternal on the higher and divine levels.*
(Paper 2:7:10, 12)

*Mortal man cannot possibly know the infinitude of the heavenly
Father. Finite mind cannot think through such an absolute truth
or fact. But this same finite human being can actually feel—
literally experience—the full and undiminished impact of such
an infinite Father's love. Such a love can be truly experienced,
albeit while quality of experience is unlimited, quantity of such
an experience is strictly limited by the human capacity for
spiritual receptivity and by the associated capacity to love the
Father in return. Finite appreciation of infinite qualities far
transcends the logically limited capacities of the creature
because of the fact that mortal man is made in the image of
God—there lives within him a fragment of infinity. Therefore
man's nearest and dearest approach to God is by and through
love, for God is love. And all of such a unique relationship is an
actual experience in cosmic sociology, the Creator–creature
relationship—the Father–child affection.* (Paper 3:4:6, 7)

*The Father desires all his creatures to be in personal communion
with him. He has on Paradise a place to receive all those whose
survival status and spiritual nature make possible such
attainment. Therefore settle in your philosophy now and
forever: To each of you and to all of us, God is approachable, the
Father is attainable, the way is open; the forces of divine love
and the ways and means of divine administration are all
interlocked in an effort to facilitate the advancement of every
worthy intelligence of every universe to the Paradise presence of
the Universal Father.* (Paper 5:1:8)

*Worship is for its own sake; prayer embodies a self- or creature-
interest element; that is the great difference between worship
and prayer. There is absolutely no self-request or other element
of personal interest in true worship; we simply worship God for*

what we comprehend him to be. Worship asks nothing and expects nothing for the worshiper. We do not worship the Father because of anything we may derive from such veneration; we render such devotion and engage in such worship as a natural and spontaneous reaction to the recognition of the Father's matchless personality and because of his lovable nature and adorable attributes. (Paper 5:3:3)

The morality of the religions of evolution drives men forward in the God quest by the motive power of fear. The religions of revelation allure men to seek for a God of love because they crave to become like him. But religion is not merely a passive feeling of "absolute dependence" and "surety of survival"; it is a living and dynamic experience of divinity attainment predicated on humanity service. (Paper 5:4:1)

You cannot truly love your fellows by a mere act of the will. Love is only born of thoroughgoing understanding of your neighbor's motives and sentiments. It is not so important to love all men today as it is that each day you learn to love one more human being. If each day or each week you achieve an understanding of one more of your fellows, and if this is the limit of your ability, then you are certainly socializing and truly spiritualizing your personality. Love is infectious, and when human devotion is intelligent and wise, love is more catching than hate. But only genuine and unselfish love is truly contagious. If each mortal could only become a focus of dynamic affection, this benign virus of love would soon pervade the sentimental emotion-stream of humanity to such an extent that all civilization would be encompassed by love, and that would be the realization of the brotherhood of man. (Paper 100:4:6)

Evil

The opposite of love is evil. In the Christian creed, evil is defined as any action or thought that goes against the will of God, the one who created this world and gave all people their seed of personality. In the dualistic approach of the Baha'i, it is not possible to cognize love without its opposite – evil. In Judaism and Islam, there is no concept of absolute evil, because God created the world, and everything that is perceived as bad has been caused by natural processes, wrongful human behavior, or purposeless activity. Buddhism considers egoism and the ensuing desires, anger and delusions to be the source of evil. Hinduism bases its assessment of evil on the concept of justice and condemns only bad acts.

Today, "evil" is defined as deliberately malicious behavior that ruins human relationships and society. Frequently, the source of evil is the injustice and distress that someone has suffered in life (usually in childhood), which stir up the desire for revenge against one's tormenters and those who observed the torment with silence or approval. But the source of evil may also be egoistic greed or a thirst for power, and the ensuing need to satisfy one's desires. An extreme form of evil is the sadistic torturing and killing of others.

Human being's express evil as envy, malice and anger. Malicious envy is apparent in the hope that other people, more successful than the envier, will meet with misfortunes that cause them material losses and emotional distress. According to the Bible, envy is one of the seven deadly sins. The word "malice" refers to action for the purpose of hatching plots against someone to damage their good name or to inflict material losses. Hate drives a person into action that is expressed in physical confrontation and battle.

The egoistic behavior model driven by desire to acquire additional profit and increase one's well-being has been the driving force for technological and economic progress and has created the world that we call modern. Actions performed for the purpose of subjugating other people can be rated favorably if the goal of these actions is to civilize uneducated people at a low level of intellectual development (i.e. driven solely by animal instincts) and teach them the practice of peaceful coexistence. However, if the goal of these egoism-driven actions is the acquisition of the fruits of another's labor, and if the subjugating activity is used to satisfy personal desires and enjoy one's feeling of superiority, it becomes evil.

What follows are some excerpts from the *Urantia Book* that deal with evil:

*God is righteous; therefore is he just. "The Lord is righteous in all his ways." "'I have not done without cause all that I have done,' says the Lord." "The judgments of the Lord are true and righteous altogether." The justice of the Universal Father cannot be influenced by the acts and performances of his creatures, "for there is no iniquity with the Lord our God, no respect of persons, no taking of gifts." ... How futile to make puerile appeals to such a God to modify his changeless decrees so that we can avoid the just consequences of the operation of his wise natural laws and righteous spiritual mandates! "Be not deceived; God is not mocked, for whatsoever a man sows that shall he also reap." True, even in the justice of reaping the harvest of wrongdoing, this divine justice is always tempered with mercy. Infinite wisdom is the eternal arbiter which determines the proportions of justice and mercy which shall be meted out in any given circumstance. **The greatest punishment (in reality an inevitable consequence) for wrongdoing and deliberate rebellion against the government of God is loss of existence** as an individual subject of that government. The final result of wholehearted sin is annihilation. In the last analysis, such sin-identified individuals have destroyed themselves by becoming wholly unreal through their embrace of iniquity. The factual disappearance of such a* *creature is, however, always delayed until the ordained order of justice current in that universe has been fully complied with. ... Undiluted evil, complete error, willful sin, and unmitigated iniquity are inherently and automatically suicidal. Such attitudes of cosmic unreality can survive in the universe only because of transient mercy-tolerance pending the action of the justice-determining and fairness-finding mechanisms of the universe tribunals of righteous adjudication.* (Paper 2:3:1–5)

Brotherhood constitutes a fact of relationship between every personality in universal existence. No person can escape the benefits or the penalties that may come as a result of relationship to other persons. The part profits or suffers in measure with the whole. The good effort of each man benefits all men; the error or evil of each man augments the tribulation of all men. As moves the part, so moves the whole. As the progress of the whole, so the progress of the part. The relative velocities of part and whole determine whether the part is retarded by the inertia of the whole or is carried forward by the momentum of the cosmic brotherhood. (Paper 12:7:11)

EVOLUTIONARY man finds it difficult fully to comprehend the significance and to grasp the meanings of evil, error, sin, and iniquity. Man is slow to perceive that contrastive perfection and imperfection produce potential evil; that conflicting truth and falsehood create confusing error; that the divine endowment of freewill choice eventuates in the divergent realms of sin and righteousness; that the persistent pursuit of divinity leads to the kingdom of God as contrasted with its continuous rejection, which leads to the domains of iniquity.

The Gods neither create evil nor permit sin and rebellion. Potential evil is time-existent in a universe embracing differential levels of perfection meanings and values. Sin is potential in all realms where imperfect beings are endowed with the ability to choose between good and evil. The very conflicting presence of truth and untruth, fact and falsehood, constitutes the potentiality of error. The deliberate choice of evil constitutes sin; the willful rejection of truth is error; the persistent pursuit of sin and error is iniquity. (Paper 54:0:1–2)

There are many ways of looking at sin, but from the universe philosophic viewpoint sin is the attitude of a personality who is knowingly resisting cosmic reality. Error might be regarded as a misconception or distortion of reality. Evil is a partial realization of, or maladjustment to, universe realities. But sin is a purposeful resistance to divine reality—a conscious choosing to oppose spiritual progress—while iniquity consists in an open and persistent defiance of recognized reality and signifies such a degree of personality disintegration as to border on cosmic insanity.

Error suggests lack of intellectual keenness; evil, deficiency of wisdom; sin, abject spiritual poverty; but iniquity is indicative of vanishing personality control. (Paper 67:1:4–5)

Iniquity in the finite domains reveals the transient reality of all God-unidentified selfhood. Only as a creature becomes God identified, does he become truly real in the universes. Finite personality is not self-created, but in the superuniverse arena of choice it does self-determine destiny. (Paper 118:7:5)

Iniquity is the willful, determined, and persistent transgression of the divine law, the Father's will. Iniquity is the measure of the continued rejection of the Father's loving plan of personality survival and the Sons' merciful ministry of salvation. (Paper 148:4:5)

But, my son, you should know that the Father does not purposely afflict his children. Man brings down upon himself unnecessary affliction as a result of his persistent refusal to walk in the better ways of the divine will. Affliction is potential in evil, but much of it has been produced by sin and iniquity. Many unusual events have transpired on this world, and it is not strange that all thinking men should be perplexed by the scenes

To hold back intentional and deliberate evil and limit the damage it causes, society has the right to demand amends for the damage caused. And if the one who committed the crime refuses, the members of society have no other alternative but to restrict the criminal's freedom of action – to remove that person from society – or lacking adequte resources, to execute that person, i.e. to send them out of this material world. This principle is propounded by the *Urantia Book*, which stresses that those people, who have deliberately and maliciously worked to reject divine love and have refused to regret their actions, shall, after the verdict is rendered, be relieved of their right to existence.

PERSONALISM

__Figure 21__. The personalistic social order exits the two-dimensional space and lays the foundation for developments in a third, i.e. spiritual dimension. The driving force for this development is the need for self-realization and its foundation is a democratic organization of society based on liberty and a market-economy environment. By: P. Tammert.

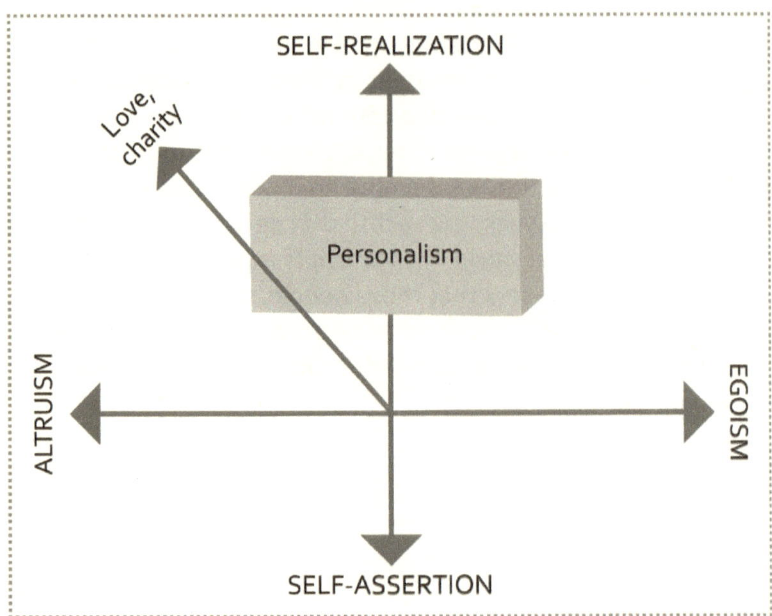

THE DEVELOPMENT OF PERSONALITY

Animals are distinguished from plants by the fact that they have sense organs and feelings arising from perceptions, and by using these they create an image of the surrounding environment. Thanks to this image, they can cognize their living environment, the dangers and opportunities inherent in it, and in the truest sense of the word to "pull up their roots" and move about independently. Only in deep sleep do animals (and humans) fall into a "vegetative state" that can be called imageless sleep.

Humans are distinguished from animals by their thinking. In the world of senses, thought is a fragment of knowledge, detached from feelings, that conveys information acquired from the surrounding reality. By gathering these fragments and stacking them next to each other, a mental image forms that allows the person to comprehend events that have taken place in the past and the relationships between them. By playing various situations through in our mind, we can experience reality ourselves without participating in it with our physical body. Furthermore, by modeling occurring processes and moving through the ensuing progress scenarios, we can imagine future developmental trends and articulate ideas that will start to change the world.

Specialization lay the foundation for market economy. Market-economy competition accelerated the furtherance of self-awareness, increased the thirst for knowledge, and paved the way for the practice of gathering and disseminating knowledge. Technological developments arising from innovation increased productivity, but egoism began shaping the evolution of society – why should one exert oneself and take risks unless there is some benefit? In the evolution of human society, this was the opening of Pandora's box. Luciferian forces (see Urantia book, Paper 53. The

Lucifer Rebellion) spilled from this vessel, taking shape as the need for self-assertion.

The first people to set out on the path of developing their personality and achieving capability of independent thought had the freedom to choose whether to apply their abilities altruistically or egoistically. The altruists became legendary tribal leaders, remembered by their nation for centuries. The egoists submitted to their desires, applying their abilities to assemble a military unit of trustworthy men, and using force to seize the property that had up to this point belonged to communities. This gave rise to the liege lords and paved the way for a class society and military state.

In market-economy societies, individualistic development continued and, in this environment, success was enjoyed by those artisans and merchants who were able to engage in cooperation in business affairs. From guilds, there developed manufactories based on division of labor and, then, factories utilizing machines. The needs created by the Industrial Revolution lay the foundation for a universal educational system, from which developed a network of vocational and technical colleges. Thanks to independent enterprise and erudition, the number of people who had set out on the path to personalistic development grew. With the increase in the number of people who were up to date with the processes taking place within society and who understood the factors that influenced these processes, the passive or active resistance to the individual-subjugating organization of society also expanded.

Today, personalistic development begins in childhood with the recognition of one's reflection in the mirror. In the course of the emergence of self-awareness that follows, the child stops talking about him- or herself in the third person and gradually begins to refer to him- or herself as "I". The next significant stage is rendering meaning to time, i.e. the words "yesterday" and "tomorrow", or past and future, and the valuation of the current moment in time.

But one does not become aware of the meaning of temporal dimensions until one understands the relationship between cause and effect through personal experience. Acquisition of knowledge and skills excites the child, who then wants to demonstrate them to everybody. During puberty, children start to defend their sovereignty, giving rise to sharp disagreements concerning their right to decide.

People do not achieve a well-developed personality until they are able to orient themselves independently in this world and achieve economic independence. Such people do not submit to manipulation by employers or "political authorities" (i.e. the opinions of dominant personalities), or to the enticements of the market-economy advertising world. Every personality is unique and capable of reshaping the surrounding reality, as there are no limits to the development of that personality's knowledge and skills. Self-awareness that is capable of development gives rise to a "virtual individual" that manages the property belonging to the individual as a legal person.

According to the *Urantia Book*, people seek power, then begin to value sovereignty, and finally demand justice. Those who have achieved a well-developed personality understand that they can offer love and service to their fellow humans; in other words, by doing good to others, they guarantee their own well-being. Those integral personalities who have reached the spiritual world can grasp the TRUTH, BEAUTY and GOODNESS that are the foundation of the Universe. (0:1:17)

THE CONCEPT OF PERSONALISM

The word "personalism" refers to an idealistic philosophical school of thought that, on the one hand, describes the uniqueness of God as the creator of the world and, on the other hand, the singularity of the personalistic person, which is particularly evident in relation to animals. The central point of this teaching is personal self-awareness – a process that occurs in the human mind upon processing the experiences gained during human self-realization. The fundamental ideas of this school of thought are:

- all personalities have unique value;
- only personalities have free will;
- only personalities are real.

The Russian religious and political philosopher Nikolai Aleksandrovich Berdyaev (1874–1948) and French theologist and essayist Emmanuel Mounier (1905–1950) have laid the foundation for this philosophical school of thought with their cultivation of the idea. Various schools of thought have developed from the further cultivation of these ideas.

- The California school of personalism was founded based on the works of moral philosopher George Holmes Howison (1834–1916) of Berkeley University.
- Philosopher and theologist Borden Parker Bowne (1847–1910), who was nominated for the Nobel Prize in Literature nine times, lay the foundation for the Boston school at Boston University.
- Polish philosopher Karol Wojtyła (1920–2005) established the Catholic school with his work entitled *Love and Responsibility*. He later became Pope John Paul II.

A personalistic social order is born when the number of people achieving a developed personality exceeds a critical limit (about 20%) in society; this prevents them from subjugating and exploiting others. When personalities, to preserve their own freedom, are forced to recognize other personalities' freedom of self-realization, they must enter into negotiation and implement the principles of democratic decision-making. This will start the development of a personalistic order.

THE FIELD OF ACTIVITY OF PERSONALISM

As mentioned above, a society based on personalities will enter a third dimension – that of spiritual fraternity – although its other aspects will remain in the material world. Thus, the personalistic social order will be shaped by three forces.

- On the axis of freedom, the field of activity of this social order will be on the side of free self-realization.
- On the axis of equality, movement should take place from right to left, based on the circumstances dominating in most states today. In the cooperativism sector, this means a transition from representative democracy to delegative- and later direct democracy, and in the individualism sector, from the capitalist model to the social market-economy model.
- On the axis of fraternity, it will mean elimination of evil, recognition of the existence of all-encompassing divine love, and the acceptance of the benefits it offers.

The characteristics of the developmental process of the personalistic social order are:

- persons who have acquired self-awareness and achieved a personalistic level of development distance themselves

from the influence of the organizations offering paternalistic guardianship and the persons who rule them;
- the state recognizes the individual's freedom of self-realization and, based upon this, the responsibility for the individual's actions and subsistence is transferred from the government (bureaucratic organization) to the individual;
- society is divided into people who have achieved a personalistic level of development and those who have not; the latter will remain under the guardianship of governmental organizations.

The people who have attained a high level of personalistic development will abandon salaried work, create their own business, operate as free enterpreneurs, or freelancer, or work as partners in commonly owned businesses. Profit-oriented businesses that pay only minimum wage for labor will no longer be able to find salaried workers in the market-economy environment, and the workers will be replaced by robots.

In modern states, the change may take place relatively peacefully, in the course of natural progress of democratization. However, transitioning to a new social order presumes radical reformation of the state's constitutional order and administrative fiats, as well as of the financial system. Changing the latter will probably be very difficult, if not impossible, because those amassing profit from the existing system will not relinquish it voluntarily.

In social states ruled by a small bureaucratic elite, the transition will take place as social cataclysms caused by uprisings organized by the masses who have enjoyed subsistence support up to this time. The cause of unrest has always been the termination of resources redistributed by the state. Rulers who are unwilling to relinquish their supremacy must be ready for "Arab Spring"-type uprisings and calls for independence by minority nationalities, as seen in the Catalan struggle for independence. And if the rulers are prepared to exercise force in order to preserve the current governmental order, this unrest will expand into civil war, and society will regress to the form of a military state.

Peaceful transition to a new social order can take place only if the proportion of personalistic persons in society has exceeded the critical limit, and they succeed in quieting the society-rending influence of the conservatives holding on to the old way of life.

Evolution in the Cooperativist Sector

On the **axis of equality**, transitioning to a personalistic social order presumes the strengthening of an altruistic way of thinking. In the organization of society, it means **greater citizen participation** in the decision-making processes that establish the legal order.

The subsistence of all individual persons, as social creatures, depends on society and its social organization. The nations who have chosen the social organization of the territorial state establish their own legal order (based on their common culture, world view or religion that has its roots in their physical and social environment and historical experience), which is formalized in the language of the ruling nation. This establishes an environment that maps out the rights and obligations of every individual, as well as their opportunities for ensuring subsistence for themselves and their family and improving their well-being. All territorial states compete among themselves for enterprising and capital-owning people, because the source of wealth is nothing other than people's work and the fruits of their labor. A state's progress is determined by how these fruits are divided among participants in the process, because those people who value the freedom of self-realization are willing to exert themselves and act creatively only if they benefit from it personally.

__Figure 22.__ The personalistic social order must distance itself from representative democracy and transition to delegative democracy, which offers all personalities the opportunity to participate in the decision-making process (if the topic applies to them), and leaves the rest of the people with the opportunity to give monetary support to an interest group, if they find that it is pursuing policy in a direction that suits them. Transition to direct democracy presumes that all people have reached a high level of personalistic development and have sufficient free time and intellectual ability to follow social discussions and express their opinions on the issues being discussed. By: P. Tammert.

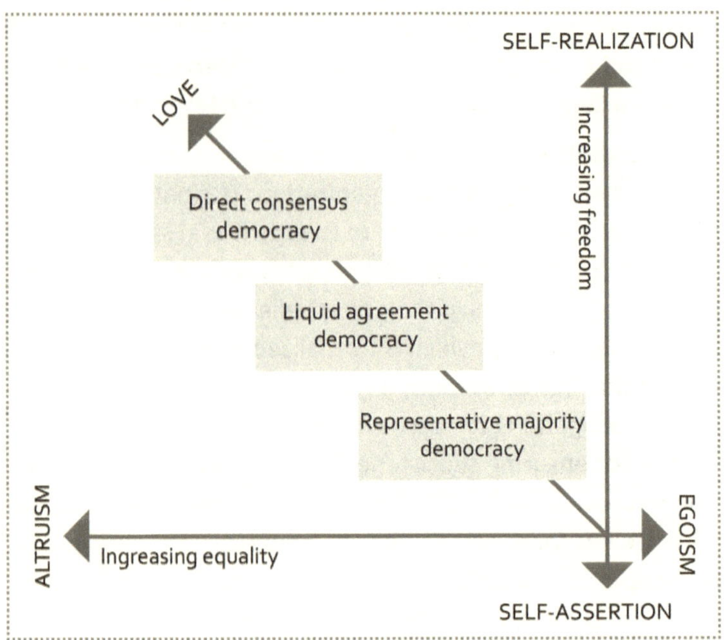

In a **representative democracy**, people surrender their right to decide to the representatives they have elected. In essence, this model of democracy is based on the traditions of the feudal society of the Middle Ages, because those with a greater number of voters who are obedient but unable to think for themselves (trained fighters) will be the winners. These winners are elected to representative bodies, but the best of them want their own kingdom to rule as sovereign! Taking advantage of the mandate they have been given, they take the position of a government minister exercising executive power, drive policies according to the interests of influential owners of capital, and turn the legislative institution into a rubber stamp. However, people who have achieved a highly developed personality want to participate in the creation of the legislation that shapes their legal order and public space, and if the proportion of these people in society increases, this model of democracy will fall into crisis.

Direct democracy might be a suitable solution, but this presumes the constant and active participation of all members of society in discussions and decision-making processes. This, in turn, presumes that all people have achieved a high level of personalistic development, and that they have sufficient time and mental strength to participate in the process. However, if most members of society are busy with the problems of everyday subsistence, and lack both education and the ability to understand the consequences of the decision under discussion, or have inadequate resources due to lack of time caused by poverty, direct democracy will fail even if voting becomes compulsory and failure to vote is punished.

The **delegative democracy** model is suitable for determination of public interests and their establishment as law in a society where the intellect of its members and their willingness to participate in the decision-making process is increasing. The premise for this model is that people will split into interest groups, and each such interest group will elect, from among themselves, an equal number of representatives to the legislative institution. Interest groups might form on the basis of a common interest, world view, ideology, or some other factor that unites people and enhances their desire to act together.

On the local level, common interests involve a territorial way of life, i.e. availability of security, infrastructure and social services. From among themselves, the residents of each territorial association elect (from one electoral district) two representatives (each monitoring the other) to the local government council, which should be large enough (60–100 members) to prevent corrupt interest groups from coming to power. In Estonia, a county would be the suitable size for a local government jurisdiction, divided into regions, each containing the same number of people (Estonian village communities are too small).

Since the body of voters in an electoral district is known, they have the right to recall their representative at any time if the representative's actions no longer satisfy the voters. This forces the representative of this community to actively engage with the voters (easily done via internet forums), to ascertain the common opinions of the community and, if needed, to obtain a mandate that will add even more clout the representative's negotiating position. If the solution is unfavorable for the community, the representative must explain to the constituency why such a decision was made. Such a principle of action would educate the voters, ease the stresses emerging during the decision-making process at the grassroots level, and give birth to a completely new kind of popular representative who knows how (and wants) to understand the needs of the voters and relate to them with empathy.

On the state level, interest groups would probably form according to economic interests, by occupations. This would mean the emergence of organizations for teachers, medical personnel, enterpreneurs, officials and others that might more accurately be called non-governmental organizations (NGOs). Every such interest group could send as many people to parliament as there are specialty committees. To limit the number of applicants, each NGO must pay its representatives a fair salary and cover the organization's management expenses. A suitable income base might be provided when every taxpayer indicates which NGO should receive 1% of the tax he or she is paying. In this case, only those NGOs that succeed in receiving enough money from such donations to cover the expenses listed above can send their representatives to the parliament.

Such an organization of government would guarantee voters the opportunity – but not the obligation – to actively participate in discussions and influence the decision-making process. If the members of the NGO are dissatisfied with the work of their representative, they would have the right to recall this person at any time. And if the actions of the NGO as a whole no longer satisfy the individual taxpayer, or the person's interest change, then the person has the right to direct 1% of their income tax to another NGO. This gives rise to an effective feedback system, and the voters retain the means of influence that help them continuously participate in the shaping of their physical and social environment. The effectiveness of the voters' own activities depends on their ability to convince and cooperate. If the term of each elected representative is limited to seven years (because the innovative ideas of any person are exhausted in the space of seven years), this will also exclude the emergence of professional politicians or, even worse, a new ruling elite.

Reforms in the decision-making process should be accompanied by reforms in the way the state is governed, with the enactment of separation of powers as articulated Charles de Montesquieu (1689-1755). In practice, this would mean that the popularly elected representatives will remain in the legislative institution and cannot exercise executive power. The judicial authority would become an independent institution that finances itself with judicial fees (stamp duty). The duty of the legislative institution would be to enforce the legal order, articulate goals, prepare and manage the budget (i.e. the Ministry of Finance should operate under the Parliament). Administrative power should be wielded by specialists in various fields, who are given the task of solving problems related to the public interest (specifying the result that they are expected to achieve) as well as the financial resources to carry them out. The organizations monitoring the officials who are paid from the state budget must also be subordinate to the legislative institution.

In the scale of the **axis of freedom**, **majority democracy** is dominant in today's democratic decision-making process; its logic of action is based on contrasting world views and ideological competition. Every party tries to limit the actions of opposing parties or even create circumstances in which they must cease operating. When most of society can understand nothing due to limited education, the politicians seeking victory in the voting process must offer their voters simple, attractive promises (along the lines of "we'll decrease taxes and increase subsidies from the state budget..."), which are never possible to fulfill in reality. The situation becomes complicated when clearly (ideologically) distinct interest groups emerge in this model of democracy, and society is polarized into opposing camps. If only two of these camps remain and they become equal in size, society falls into crisis, increasing the threat of civil war. This, in turn, harms the well-being of society and destroys the global competitiveness of the territorial state.

Because delegative democracy is based on interest groups, it cannot operate on the principle of majority democracy. Imagine what would happen if teachers or officials begin to oppress doctors by taking away all the finances they need for their work, or if doctors take away all the finances of farmers. Because decisions such as these would hurt the decision-makers themselves, leaving them without medical care or food, participants in the process must transition to the principle of **contract (agreement) democracy**, enter into lengthy negotiations (sometimes maliciously called "horse-trading"), and seek a compromise that will satisfy all parties. In this process, everyone loses, but they lose so little that it does not hurt their subsistence and offers an opportunity to continue working together.

Society will achieve **consensus democracy** only when most members of society (at least 80–90%) have achieved a high level of personalistic development. This means that people will no longer need employers who tell them what they must do to receive the money needed for subsistence, or the paternalistic care of officials who enact lists of prohibited activities and punish those who fail to abide by it. Such a pacifistic (peace-loving) organization of society can emerge only on a global scale, because as long as a nation or state leader dreams of acquiring the natural resources held by another nation or the fruits of the labors of other people, the transition to the principle of consensus democracy is not possible.

In summary. Transitioning the rule of a territorial state to the principles of delegative democracy and complete separation of powers would bring about the following positive changes:

- abandoning representative and majority democracy will bring an end to political parties' "feudal army" logic of operations and will open the way for improving social well-being;
- the need to spend millions of dollars on election campaigns and public opinion polls would cease to exist;

- if the executive authority loses its right to create legislation, and party leaders in the position of government minister can no longer manipulate members of the legislative body (the rubber-stamp phenomenon), opportunities for political corruption would diminish abruptly;
- the populist base, i.e. the need for candidates to make promises to voters who live on government subsidies that can never be fulfilled in reality, will cease to exist;
- the opportunity to create rifts in society and manipulate a society polarized along the lines of world view will no longer exist;
- opportunities for self-realization will improve for those who are competent in their field, and diminish for those who put on an honest face to lie to the people;
- the risk of the development of a new hereditary elite class will diminish.

Recalling the "smart swarm" phenomenon, an organization of society based on delegative democracy could offer society better opportunities for sustainable development. A democratic system of governance would be further enhanced by the decision-making process known as sociocracy, in which first the problem is ascertained and then a solution is sought. After finding the solution, it is put into action, and in the case of several competing solutions, they are put to a vote, and the solution receiving the most votes is implemented. Voting against any of them is not allowed, because this will cause rifts in society and offer up a malicious opportunity to obstruct implementation of the changes.

Evolution in the Individualistic Sector

**Figure 23**. An inevitable presumption for the transition to a personalistic social order is the ability of people to restrain their egoistic greed for profit. At the start of the road to personalism, society must implement the social market economy model that will offer maximum opportunities to anyone who wishes and is able to advance (i.e. opportunities for study, a healthy living environment and a free market). Movement toward a free-market model cannot begin until the proportion of personalistic people in society exceeds 50%. By: P.Tammert.

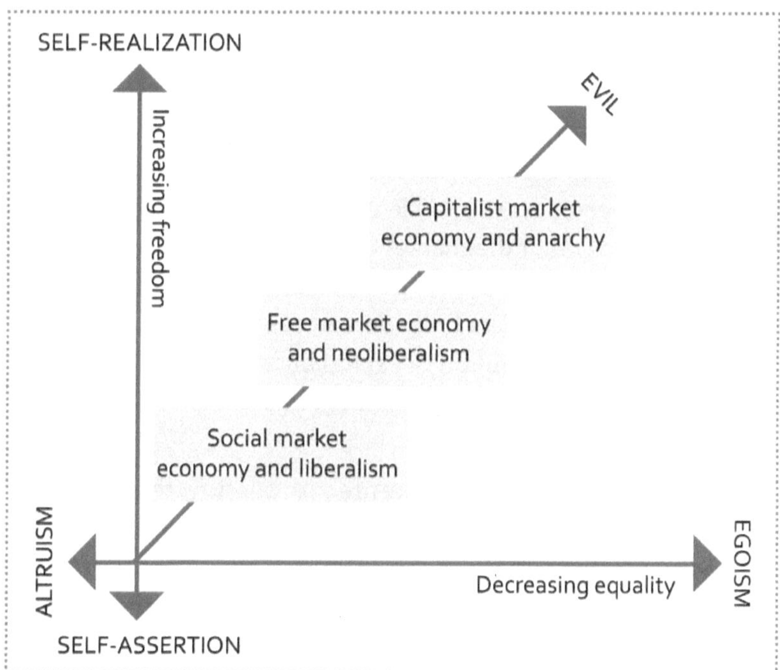

On the **axis of equality**, transitioning to the personalistic social order presumes the weakening of egoistic motives in economic activity. Let us recall that a market economy is based on specialization and exchange transactions for the purpose of acquiring income. If the income collected by the seller does not cover production costs, this person will lose the (private) property that represents the foundation of their freedom, and they will become someone's vassal or slave. It makes no difference at all whether this happens because of deception caused by someone's greed for profit or from an altruistic desire to help others.

Followers of the **capitalistic economic model** based on egoism value only the size of the profit, and care nothing about the nature of the transactions that were made for its acquisition or the resulting consequences. In everyday life, this means that transactions are based on the interests of the capital owners and are made unfairly, causing damage to the transactional environment. In these circumstances, profit and property come into the hands of an ever-narrowing circle of individuals, allowing increased manipulation of the market by the owners of capital. This leads to an ever-increasing part of the population becoming dependent on their employers or lenders of capital. When unequal market relations and distribution of capital become fixed, it causes a stratification of society and opens the way for the loss of the market-economy order.

As John Locke noted in the seventeenth century, the driving force for market economy is the right of the person to decide for oneself and to enjoy the fruits of one's labors in the form of private property. This is possible only if each market participant is guaranteed an equal opportunity to obtain the resources needed for economic activity, and to sell the fruits of one's labors on the market. However, since there will always be people who want to redistribute income and take away the property belonging to others, market-economy freedoms must be protected by implementation of governmental coercive force and prevention of malicious attempts to limit market freedoms.

The **free market-economy model** offers everyone maximum opportunities for self-realization; however, the extent to which each person is able (and wants to) take advantage of the existing opportunities is up to that person alone. And, since every person has vastly different inherited abilities and will to achieve, the outcome of each person's activities will also be vastly different. However, in contrast to capitalist market economy, the winners in this economic model can never take a rest or enjoy the benefits of the acquired wealth, because market-economy processes are relentless in their continuity. New technological inventions and technologies create new opportunities, and those people who continue to hold on to the old ways can lose everything they have.

The most altruistic is the **social market-economy model**, which, in promoting competitive ability within the market-economy environment of a company or state, places the greatest value on the economic progress of society as a whole, or the state that represents it, and considers the need to ensure its sustainability of greater importance than the right of all individuals to consume equally. This means that officials representing public interests have not only the right to limit individual freedom of activity, if the actions of such individuals endanger social order or damage the physical or social environment, but also to redistribute the profit they earn by using mechanisms of the tax and budget system. By offering education to the people who want it, according to their abilities, and maximizing their opportunities for self-realization, society will continue to improve its competitive edge and increase subsistence opportunities for all its members. Those who are unable to learn anything and do not wish to do anything will remain under the guardianship of the officials, i.e. they will be offered minimal subsistence opportunities in circumstances of limited freedom of activity.

In the scale of the **axis of freedom**, the market-economy environment is shaped by three concepts of freedom and the ideologies that represent them.

The concept of **negative freedom** denies the right of officials representing the elite to limit the freedom of business activities and interfere in economic processes. But understanding the public interest of the state, entrepeneurs recognize the right of officials to interfere in economic processes. In the social market-economy model, this means using the taxation system to collect money into the state budget, which is then used to establish a safe and healthy physical and social environment and distribution of subsidies to those who wish to advance themselves and use this advancement to offer society something in return. In the free market-economy model, the actions of officials are limited to the shaping of the legal space and imposing sanctions on those whose actions have violated market freedoms or damaged other people's property or subsistence, and thereby the competitiveness of all of society. In the capitalistic market-economy model, officials become corrupt and start cooperating with the owners of capital in pursuit of their own self-interest. The conditions for these developments are created by the mindset of society and paltry salaries for the officials.

The world view based on the concept of **positive freedom** originates from the interests of entrepreneurial personalities. In the case of the social market economy model it means mutually beneficial cooperation, require everyone to adhere to free-market principles, and limit transactions with individuals whose actions hurt the subsistence of business partners. In the free market-economy model, reciprocally taking the interests of others into account expands to encompass the globe, with a concurrent intensification of interstate competition. In the capitalistic market-economy model, there is a drive for maximum profit, giving rise to a struggle for existence in which only the strongest and most ignoble survive.

The concept of **individualistic freedom** is based on the anarchist world view and follows the pacifist behavior model. In the social market-economy environment, it is founded on voluntary cooperation between individuals. This may take place as joint endeavors of private enterpreneurs (cooperatives), with the goal of improving one's position in market-economy competition, or as an employees' syndicate, in which a company's workers organize themselves and together manage the economic activities of a large enterprise (for example, Great Britain's John Lewis Partnership, which is the country's second-largest retail chain with its 51 department stores and Waitrose shops). In the free market-economy model, it is very difficult to preserve a sustainable environment for progress, because when its participants focus only on material self-realization, society will polarize and focus on serving its own egoistic interests. Because the same process intensifies even more in the capitalistic market-economy model, the total concentration of property and the weakness (corruption) of the regulating state authority could pave the way for disturbances and the spread of violence in society.

In summary. The developmental potential of personalism as a social order is determined by how many people in the society have achieved a high level of personalistic development, and how great is their ability to cooperate with each other without outside intervention. Because personalities are economically independent and non-manipulable, the increase of their numbers in society begins to proportionally limit the opportunities of greedy people to redistribute the fruits of others' labor. This in turn causes the decline of the capitalistic economic model and, depending on the strength of the altruistic way of thinking, transition to the free market or social free market model. If the society wants to remain at the forefront of global competition, it must choose a more altruistic social market-economy model, and offer its more talented young people maximum opportunities for improvement and self-realization, and limit its spending on those who cannot or will not make an effort. However, if society is more egoistic, placing individual self-realization higher than the progress of the state as a whole, it will choose the free market-economy model. Everyone's options are more plentiful on the axis of freedom, because the conception of freedom that one wants and is able to follow depends on that person's level of development and personal character.

Evolution on the axis of fraternity

First of all, let us remember that the approach to the concept of **fraternity** as presented here is based on the *Urantia Book* and, in this context, fraternity ensues from fully developed integral personalities and the respect they have for each other. The word **love** denotes the desire to do good to others.

When people achieve the level of integral personality and understand the consequences of evil (envy, malice and hate) and how they affect people themselves as well as all of society, they may finally comprehend that, in the long run, it is better to do good to others. A personality reaches a completely new level of development when one becomes aware of the existence of the spiritual world and the prevailing fraternity of the spiritual beings who dwell there. In the context of the *Urantia Book*, this means that people recognize the existence of a spiritual being who create the Universe, and that they have been given the seed of personality, which, when cultivated, allows progress from one level of development to the next, and from one planet world to another. During one's developmental process, people realize that they have been given a Thought Adjuster to help them; an entity who helps solve difficult problems and offers guidance in critical situations, keeps watch over them, and informs the spiritual world of their thoughts and feelings. The report of the Thought Adjuster determines the person's further opportunities for development in future existences.

The idea that the Universe has consciousness is borne throughout the *Urantia Book*; nothing happens "just because", by chance. In his book *Up From Eden* (1981), American Kenneth Earl *alias* Ken Wilber (born 1949), founder of transpersonal psychology, describes the birth of the human ego and its progress from Universal preconsciousness through self-awareness to superconsciousness, and the effects of various stages of development on this process. Because the development of human consciousness through the millennia can neither be studied directly nor described on the basis of empirical data, it must be done hermeneutically, i.e. by evaluating the nature of things and interpreting the meaning of the footprints of mental activity.

As we study the historical evolution of nations and states, we can see that their progress ceases when their rulers, driven either by greed or excessive good will, have taken away their subjects' liberty to make independent choices, make mistakes, and accept the consequences. The outcome is even worse if the ruler attempts to forcibly lead the people into a well-being society by subjugating them to his will. Once the freedom of self-realization and opportunity to acquire profit is lost, creativity is also lost, and the entire nation or state loses its chance to participate in global progress. It is also true that nobody has succeeded in creating a well-being society in which the leader and governing officials do all the people's work for them, and the citizens simply have the right to demand ever greater benefits. Such attempts fail because it is the labor or sacrifice of these citizens that must provide the source of these benefits. It is true that additional resources could be taken from other countries or nations, but that would require the use of force and disruption of global progress. In a word: there is no such thing as a free lunch, and those who want something for free must sacrifice their own freedom of self-realization and right to choose, as well as the fruits of their own labor.

A new, fraternity-based social order will emerge when people abandon the materialistic world view that limits cognitive power, and leave behind the religions that sow fear and demand submission, recognize the existence of the spiritual world that values self-realization, and let their intellect enter into a personal relationship with the one who has given them the seed of their personality. The behavior of a loving personality expresses respect, regardless of the other personality's nature and level of development, and focuses on serving the basic values (TRUTH, BEAUTY and GOODNESS) of the Universe.

The development of spiritual fraternity on our planet is most severely obstructed by the conventional culture that is the consequence of a nation's historical fate, physical and social environment, and world view, and their language-based legal order, which distinguishes the people living in territorial states from each other. Differences arising from climatic conditions and natural environment will remain, and those we cannot change; however, we can diminish their influence on our activities as we continue making technological progress. The crimes committed by other nations and states can finally be forgotten or forgiven, and bad practices can be changed, leaving only those having a rational basis and helping improve our daily subsistence. Spiritual development will make progress when people become free from the influence of religions that sow fear, and adopt the fundamental values that reign in the Universe.

The greatest obstacle on the road to spiritual fraternity is language-based legal order. This obstacle cannot be overcome until humankind adopts new ways of communication. The first step toward this goal has been the implementation of the Internet and social media (Facebook, Twitter, Skype, Messenger, etc.), which allow free communication globally. The next important step will be the implementation of machine translation programs (Google, Microsoft, etc.). Transition to voice-recognition computer communications (Siri, Cortana, Amazon Alexa, etc.) will render keyboards obsolete; they will probably become obsolete during the next decade. This will change the legislation that is, by nature, the foundation of the legal order, because few people would be able to grasp the meaning of a law comprising thousands of sections (e.g. Law of Obligations), or understand, let alone abide by, legislative acts peppered with references.

A completely new developmental dimension will be opened up by image-based communication, for which the groundwork has already been laid by Instagram. Science news already reports that by reading electrical signals from the brain, computers can ascertain the thoughts that are forming even before the person expresses them in words. As these developments continue, spoken language will also become obsolete, and people will communicate by exchanging thought images. After that, we need to take only one small step to reach the level of transcendental superconsciousness described by Ken Wilber, in which interpersonal communication is based on emotion-charged intellectual images, conveying meaning without the use of language or technical equipment. If that ever becomes reality, it will be the one thing that lays the foundation for the emergence of global spiritual fraternity. This will bring an end to the era of territorial states that have imposed their own legal order throughout human history.

SUMMARY

In the center of the approach to history and society presented in this book is the spiritual person. In *Up from Eden*, Ken Wilber describes the development of human self-consciousness from primeval times onward and expresses the opinion that original sin was actually the individualization of the person, i.e. the person separated from the spiritual source or the common consciousness of the Universe, acquiring self-awareness and intellectual imagination. The more precisely a person is able to reflect the surrounding reality in one's mind, the more independent one becomes. The process achieves its goal when the person's mental image overlaps with reality to the extent that one begins to understand the relationships between cause and effect. There develops a personality who perceives the environment, is an independent actor and creator, and has the ability to change the prevailing reality.

When personalities are few and they think altruistically, they become great tribal leaders. Personalities driven by egoism become warlords whose goal is the satisfaction of their personal greed and need to subjugate others. As the number of warlords increases, they must share power and elect a king from their midst. That is how the elitarian governmental culture is born.

When people specialize in manufacturing or trading of goods and begin taking responsibility for their own subsistence and that of their families, they set out on the path to personalistic development. From free market-economy exchange emerges economic democracy, which eventually extends to the entire organization of society. Because the outcome of international and interstate competition depends on the population's educational level, improvement of educational systems becomes a priority and compulsory education becomes universal. Personalistic development is boosted by raising the level of knowledge, increasing specialization, and individualizing work obligations. During the first industrial revolutions, rural workers became factory workers whose dependency on their employers grew, but the Fourth Industrial Revolution turned these developments upside-down. Advances in technology and specialized knowledge have made the owners of big business dependent on top specialists in their fields. And even more importantly: new technologies allow one-man operations to make products that could previously be manufactured only by companies with large factories. This creates unprecedented opportunities for independent enterpreneurship. It leads to an increase in the proportion of economically independent enterpreneurs in the population. These people have a competent understanding of their environment. Rulers, collaborating with the media, cannot manipulate their opinions, and advertisement fails to entice them.

A new qualitative developmental stage for human society will begin when the proportion of people achieving a high level of personalistic development rises above about 20% and their authority grows so great that their companions start taking the opinions of these personalities into account when making their decisions. In everyday life, this will appear first as the lack of salaried labor. People who can orient themselves in their environment and are able to resolve the issues of their subsistence themselves no longer need the protectorship of employers or rulers. The next crisis will take shape as the disappearance of the current religious organizations and party memberships, and the birth of new political movements. This represents the efforts of personalistic people to find new forms of cohabitation and new ways of organizing society. In this book, the attempt was made to describe one potential solution, in the form of citizen society and personalistic social order.

Thanks to all my readers for the time and attention you have devoted to this book!

REFERENCES

Acemoglu, Daron; Robinson, James a. Why Nations Fail. The Origins of Power, Prosperity, and Poverty. Crown Business, 2012

Anderson, Christopher J., Christine A. Guillory (1997). "Political Institutions and Satisfaction with Democracy: A Cross-National Analysis of Consensus and Majoritarian Systems." – American Political Science Review 91, no. 1 (March), lk 66-81. http://www.jkarp.com/2007_08/Anderson_1997.pdf (01.10.2015)

Annus, Amer; Kaspar Kolk, Jaan Puhvel, Janika Päll. Muinasaja seadusekogumike antoloogia. Varrak, 2001

Beckert, Jens. International Encyclopedia of Economic Sociology, Routlege, 2011

Benda-Beckmann, Keebet von; Pirie Fernanda. Order and Disorder. Antropological Perspectives. Berghahn Books. 2007

Berger, L. Peter. The Capitalist spirit. Institute for Contemporary Studies San Francisco, 1990

Berger, L. Peter. Social construction of reality : a treatise in the sociology of knowledge, Penguin Books, 1991

Berlin, Isiah. Two concepts of liberty. Oxford University Press, 1958. http://cactus.dixie.edu/green/B_Readings/I_Berlin%20Two%20Concpets%20of%20Liberty.pdf (11.07.2019)

Bloom, Howard. The Lucifer principle. A Scientific expedition into the forces of History. The Atlantic Monthly Press, 1995

Breton, Denise; Lehman, Stephen. The Mystic Heard of Justice. Chrysalis Books, 2001

Bronner, Stephen Eric, Critical Theory, Oxford University Press, 2011

Burke, Peter. Mis on kultuuriajalugu? TLÜ Kirjastus, 2011 (orig 2004)

Cartledge, Paul. Democracy, A Life. Oxford University Press, 2016

Chai, Sun-Ki. Explaining Social Order and Norms of Cooperation: Nested Hierarchies. http://www2.hawaii.edu/~sunki/paper/solgame.pdf (15.03.2016)

Child, John. Hierarchy, Akay Idea for Business and Society, Routlege, 2019.

Chini, Chiara; Moroni, Sheyla. Populism, A Historiographic Category? Cambridge Scholars Publishing, 2018

Clausewitz, Carl von. Sõjast. Eesti Keele Sihtasutus, 2004 (orig 1832)

Collier, Paul. The Future of Capitalism. Harper Collins Publishers, 2018

Davies, Glyn. A History of Money. From Ancient Times to the Present Day. University of Wales Press, 1994

Diamond, Larry. In search of Democracy. Routledge, 2016

Dijk, Teun A. van. Ideoloogia multidistsiplinaarne käsitlus. TÜ Kirjastus, 2005 (orig 1998)

Dunleavy, Patrick; O'Leary, Brendan. Riigiteooriad: Liberaalse demokraatia poliitika. Külim, 1995 (orig 1992)

Eco, Umberto. Five moral pieces. Harcourt Books, 2002 (orig 1997)

Erhard, Ludwig. Heaolu kõigile. (Prosperity for all. Wohlstand für Alle). ECON Verlag GmbH, 1998 (orig 1957)

Erhard, Ludwig. Saksan ihme. Gummerus, 1959

Ertman, Thomas. Birth of the Leviathan. Building States and Regimes in Medieval and Early Modern Europe. The University of Cambridge Press, 1997

Ferguson, Niall. Raha võidukäik. (The Ascent of Money). Varrak, 2010

Ford, Bryan. Delegative Democracy. http://www.brynosaurus.com/deleg/ (25.09.2015)

Ford, Henry. Minu elu ja töö. Loodus, 1938 (orig 1922)

Friedman, Milton. Kapitalism ja vabadus. Eesti Avatud Ühiskonna Instituut, 1994 (orig 1982)

Fulcher, James. Capitalism. A very Short Introduction. Oxford University Press, 2004

Geertz, Clifford. The Interpretation of Cultures, Basic Books, 1073

Giddens, Anthony. The Third way, The Renewal of Social Democracy Polity Press, 1998

Glete, Jan. War and State. Routledge, 2002

Goff, Jaques le. Raha või elu. Prantsuse Kultuurikeskus, 2001 (orig 1986)

Greve, Bent. Social and Labour Market Policy, the basics. Routlege, 2018

Hale, Henry E. Patronal Politics. Cambridge University Press, 2015

Hart, H.L.A. The Concept of Law. Oxford University Press, 2012

Hattenhauer, Hans. Euroopa õigusajalugu. Juura, 2007 (orig 2004)

Hawking, Stephen. Universum pähklikoores. Eesti Entsüklopeedia-kirjastus, 2002 (orig 2001)

Hayek, Friedrich. "Cosmos and Taxis" – Theories of Social order. Stanford University, 2009

Hayek, Friedrich. Individualism and Economic order. The University of Chicago Press, 1948 (orig 1948)

Hechter, Michael; Horne, Christine. Theories of Social order. Stanford University, 2009

Heidenheimer, Arnold J.; Heclo, Hugh; Adams, Carolyn Teich. Võrdlev halduspoliitika. Külim, 1995 (orig 1990)

Hiob, Arne. Martin Luther ja protestantlik reformatsioon. Johannes Esto Kirjestus. 2017

Holiday, Ryan, Ego is the enemy. Penguin Random House LLC, 2016

Hood, Christopher. The Art of The State. Culture, Rhethoric, and Public Management. Oxford University Press, 2000

Howard, Michael. Rahu leiutamine. Eesti Entsüklopeediakirjastus, 2006 (orig 2000)

Huntington, Samuel P. Tsivilisatsioonide kokkupõrge. Fontes, 1999 (orig 1996)

Juntune, Hannu. Oikeuden idean teologiset perustet. Kauppakaari OY, 2000

Jõgi, Piibe. Õigus ja eetika. Teooriaid õiglusest ja eetikast 20. sajandi õigusfilosoofias. Juura, 1997

Kaplow, Louis; Shavell, Steven. Fairness versus Welfare. Harvard University Press, 2002

Kaspersen, Lars Bo and Strandsbjerg Jeppe. Does War Make States? Cambridge University Press, 2017

Kaufmann, Bruno; Biichi, Rolf; Braun, Nadja. The IRI Guidbook to Direct Democracy. Initiative & Referndum Institute, 2007

Keegan, John. Sõjakunsti ajalugu. Varrak, 2004

Keynes, John Maynard. The General Theory of Employment, Interest and Money, Macmillan&Co, 1936

Knowles, Dudley. Hegel and the Philosophy of Right. Routlege, 2002

Koraan. Tõlk Haljand Udam. AS Bit 2007

Korppinen, Pekka. Valtio ja vapauden kasvu. Hakapaino OY, 1989

Kramer, Samuel Noah. Histrory Begins at Sumer. Thirty-nine firsts in recorded history. University of Pennsylvania Press, 1981

Krinal, Valner. Majandusteaduse ajaloost. TÜ Kirjastus, 1998

Kuehnelt-Leddihn, Erik. Demokraatia analüüs. Andro Kitus ja EYS Veljesto, 2004 (orig 1995)

Käsitteet liikkeessä. Kokoelma Suomen poliititsen kultuuri käsitehistoriasta. Vastapaino, 2003

Laurinkari, Juhani. Yhteisötalous. Gaudeamus, 2007

Lane-Mercier, Gillian; Merkle Denise; Koustas Jane. Minority Languages, National Langages, and Official Languages Policies. McGill-Queen's University Press, 2018

Lessenoff, Michael H. The Spirit of Capitalism and the Protestant Ethic. An Enquiry into the Weber thesis. University of Glasgow, Edward Elgar Publishing Ltd 1994

Lietaer, Bernard. The Future of Money. Random House Groub Ltd, 2001

Lijphart, Arend. Demokraatia mustrid. Eesti Rahvusraamatukogu, 2009 (orig 1999)

Lindbeck, Assar. The growth of government. Nobel symposium 61. Journal of Public Economics vol. 28, issue 3, December 1985, lk 273. http://www.sciencedirect.com/science/article/pii/00472727859 00593 (12.12.2016)

Locke, John. Teine traktaat valitsemisest. Essee tsiviilvalitsuse tegelikust algusest, ulatusest ja eesmärgist. Kultuurileht, 2007 (orig 1698)

Luhmann, Niklas. Sotsiaalsed süsteemid. Ilmamaa, 2009 (orig 1984)

Lõhmus, Uno. Õigusriik ja inimese õigused. Ilmamaa, 2018

Machiavelli, Niccolo. Valitseja. Avatud Eesti Fond, 2001 (orig 1513)

Madisson, Agnus. Contours of World Economy. Oxford University
    Press, 2007

Mahoney, James; Thelen, Kathleen. Explaining Institutional Change.
    Ambiguity, Agency, and Power. Cambridge University Press, 2009

Mann, Michael. The Sources of Social Power. Cambridge University
    Press, 1986

Meadows, Donella & Dennis; Randers, Jorgen. Kasvun rajat. 30
    vuotta myöhemmin. Gaudeamus, 2005 (orig 2004)

Mill, John Stuart. Vabadusest. Hortus Litterarum, 1996 (orig 1859)

Miller, David. Political philosophy. Oxford University Press, 2003

Miller, Peter. Tark parv. Äripäeva raamatuklubi, 2011 (orig 2010)

Mises, Ludwig von. Liberalism. Ilmamaa, 2007 (orig 1927)

Moisi, Dominique. Emotsioonide geopoliitika. Eesti Päevalehe AS,
    2010 (orig 2009)

Moller, Jorgen. State Formation, Regime Change, and Economic
    Development. Routlege, 2017

Montesquieu, Charles de. The spirit of laws. 1899.
    https://archive.org/details/spiritoflaws01montuoft (22.02.2016)

Murphy, Liam; Nagel Thomas. The Myth of Ownership. Taxes and
    Justice. Oxford University Press. 2002

Nikulin, Dimitri The Concept of History , Bloomsbury Academic
    Publishing Plc, 2017

Norberg, Johan. Inimeste rikkus – globaalne turumajandus. Eesti
    Entsüklopeediakirjastus, 2003 (orig 2001)

North, Douglass C. Institutsioonid, institutsiooniline muutus ja
    majandusedu. Fontes, 1990 (orig 1990)

Oleinik, Anton. Reforming the State without Changing the Model of
Power? On Administrative Reform in Post-Socialist Countries.
Routlege, 2009

Palan, Ronen. Global Political Economy. Contemporary theories.
Routledge, 2000

Parson, Wayne. Public Policy. Edward Elgar Publishing Ltd, 1995

Platon. Teosed: I köide. Avatud Eesti raamat, Ilmamaa, 2003

Potter, Karl. Avatud ühiskond ja selle vaenlased. Platoni lummus.
Avatud Eesti Fond, 2010 (orig 1945)

Proudhon, Pierre-Joseph. General Idea of the Revolution in the
Nineteenth Century (1851), http://fair-use.org/p-j-
proudhon/general-idea-of-the-revolution/ (15.05.2016)

Putnam, Robert. Üksi keeglisaalis. Hermes, 2008 (orig 2000)

Raud, Rein. Mis on kultuur. Sissejuhatus kultuuriteooriasse. Eesti
keele sihtasutus, TLÜ Kirjastus, 2013

Ricardo, David. The principles of political economy and taxation.
Dutton, 1923 (orig 1817)

Rodrik, Dani. The Globalization Paradox. Why Global markets, States
and Democracy can't coexist. Oxford University Press, 2011

Rothbard, Murray N. Economic Thought Before Adam Smith. An
Austrian Perspective on the History of Economic Thought
Volume I. Edward Elgar Publishing Ltd., 1995

Rousseau, Jean-Jaques. Ühiskondlikust lepingust ehk riigiõiguse
põhiprintsiibid. Varrak, 1998 (orig 1762)

Sarrazin, Thilo. Saksamaa käib maha. Ohtlik mäng oma riigiga. Hea
lugu OÜ, 2013 (orig 2010)

Scruton, Roger. How to be a Conservative. Bloomsbury Publishing,
2014

Sen, Amartya. "Utilitarianism and Welfarism" – The Journal of Philosophy, Vol. 76, No. 9, 1979, lk 463-489

Sen, Amartya. The Idea of Justice. Allen Lane, 2009

Siddiqi, Muhammad Nejatullah. Muslim Economic Thinking. The Islamic Foundation. University of Cambridge Press, 1998

Skidelsky, Robert. Keynes, the return of the Master. Allen Lane, 2009

Smil, Vaclav, Energy and Civilization. A History. The MIT Press, 2017

Smith, Adam. Uurimus riikide rikkuse ja iseloomu põhjustest. Ilmamaa, 2005 (orig 1776)

Spengler, Oswald. Õhtumaa allakäik. Ilmamaa, 2007 (orig 1918)

Stein, Walter Johannes. Gold & Labour in History and in Modern Times. St George Publications, 1986

Steinmo, Seven. Kathleen Thelen, Frank Longstreth. Historical Institutionalism in Comparative Analysis, 1992. https://www.jstor.org/stable/2132374?seq=1#page_scan_tab_c ontents (15.04.2016)

Struve, V. V. Vana-Idamaade ajalugu. RK Teaduslik kirjandus, 1949 (orig 1941)

Sutherland, Douglas. The Landowners. Anthony Blond Ltd, 1968

Tennmann, Eduard. Usk ja majandus. Noor-Eesti Kirjastus, 1938 (orig 1938)

Tocqueville, Alexis de. On Democracy in America. Hortus Litterarium, 1995 (orig 1874)

Tolonen, Hannu. Korko, raha ja sopimus. Korkokielto ja sen hviäminen rahan sekä pääoman syntymisen ongelmana. Lakimiesliiton Kustannus. 1992

Urantia. Urantia Foundation, 2010 (orig 1955)

Weber, Max. General economic history. Collier Books, 1961 (orig 1923)

Weber, Max. Protestantlik eetika ja kapitalismi vaim. Varrak, 2007 (orig 1991)

Vernant, Jean-Pierre. Vana-Kreeka inimene. Avita, 2001 (orig 1991)

Wilber, Ken. Eedenist alates. Eesti Transpersonaalne Assotsiatsioon, 2014 (orig 1981)

Wildavsky, Aaron ja Carolyn Webber. A History of Taxation and Budgeting in the Western World. New York: Simon & Schuster, 1986

Winkiel, Laura, Modernism, the basics. Routlege, 2017

Wright, Georg Henrik von. Humanism as an Approach to Life. Otava, 1998 (orig 1978)

www.ingramcontent.com/pod-product-compliance
Lightning Source LLC
Chambersburg PA
CBHW031059250726
48655CB00004B/1509